The English Legal System

A concise introduction for students

Studymates

Many other titles in preparation

The English Legal System

A concise introduction for students

Dr Stephen T Hardy
JP LLB PhD

Lecturer in Law, University of Salford

Studymates

Dedication
To P. Richard Stevens of Stevens Solicitors, Stoke on Trent. With thanks and much appreciation for your advice and guidance and for igniting and maintaining my interest in the English legal system

First published in 1999 by Studymates, a Division of International Briefings Ltd, Unit 5 Dolphin Building, Queen Anne's Battery, Plymouth PL4 0LP, United Kingdom

Customer services tel:	(01752) 202301
Orders fax:	(01752) 202333
Web site:	http://www.studymates.co.uk
Customer services email:	cservs@plymbridge.com
Editorial email:	publisher@studymates.co.uk
Distributors web site:	http://www.plymbridge.com

Origination by PDQ Typesetting, Newcastle-under-Lyme, Staffordshire.
Printed and bound by The Cromwell Press Ltd, Trowbridge, Wiltshire.

Contents

Contents

List of Illustrations

Preface

According to Glanville Williams: 'Law is the cement of society and an essential medium of change. A knowledge of law increases one's understanding of public affairs. Its study promotes accuracy of expression, facility in argument and skill in interpreting the written word, as well as understanding of social values.' (*Learning the Law*, p.1).

To promise in this text to cover all of Williams' observations would be rather too ambitious. However, such a statement is as true now as when it was first written in 1945. Although, our society has dramatically changed over the last fifty or so years, so has law. In fact, law has greatly helped in the reshaping of our society. With this observation and the testament from Williams in mind, this book aims both to direct the study and to stimulate the learning of the student of law from whatever background, discipline or motive. Like William's learned introductory exposition of law, this text aims to be both a 'guide' and studymate to the reader.

The topic of 'the English Legal System' covers a vast area. The system has been shaped by history, politics, economics, sociology and legal developments, as well as by philosophical theory. Consequently, to understand it the student needs some knowledge of the many disciplines which interact with and make up this phenomenon known as the 'English Legal System' (ELS).

No doubt as we enter an extraordinary new age, further changes and challenges will confront the English legal system. Keeping abreast of these, and understanding the underlying principles, makes for a good foundation in legal knowledge.

I wish to thank those who taught me 'ELS' at UCL, as an undergraduate (especially Professor M D A Freeman) and to acknowledge the kind assistance of Martin Hannibal, Michelle Brooks (secretarial) and Roger Ferneyhough (publisher), as well as the many colleagues and law students I have worked with and taught, and from whom I have learned so much over the past years.

I dedicate this book to Richard Stevens (Solicitor) who was kind enough to introduce me to the English legal system, forensically, and to start my long walk along the pathway to law, as a work experience student some fourteen years ago. For that, I will be eternally grateful.

As ever, I thank Louise for her love and patience in allowing this project to be completed. Any errors and omissions contained in this text are solely the responsibility of the author.

The law is stated as at 31st August 1999.

Stephen Hardy

1

Studying Law Today

One minute summary – In this chapter we introduce the nature of law and its importance to society. It will show you how to categorise law, how to understand the British legal framework and the fundamental principles of the rule of law and separation of powers. Also, you will learn how to use a law library and read a law report, and how to obtain some basic and important legal skills. In this chapter we will explore:

▶ introducing law
▶ categories of law
▶ the rule of law
▶ the separation of powers
▶ theories of law
▶ the law library
▶ reading law reports
▶ legal skills

Introducing law

The 'English legal system' is a vital part of every law student's course. However, law students are not always aware of the social context in which the rules of law they are studying will actually operate. Some are apt to ignore matters of study which they think are better left to social scientists – such topics as the institutions, processes and personnel of the English legal system. Don't make this mistake!

Almost every aspect of life in the UK – as in any state – is regulated or affected in some way by law. There are laws to provide for the remedying of grievances. There are laws to prohibit anti-social activities, and to impose penal sanctions for their breach.

There are laws to regulate potentially harmful activities. For example we have systems for licensing, registration or inspection, usually in conjunction with the prescription of standards. There are laws which confer state benefits upon individuals, and there are laws which facilitate private arrangements. The whole body of English law could be said to constitute the 'English legal system'.

Legal labels

Any legal system has within it many different labels. These are used every day by those who take part in the system. These labels also often confuse students of law. The most used labels in a British context are:

(a) the English legal system
(b) the common law

The label 'English legal system' is a convenient one, but we need to treat it with a little care. For one thing, it extends only to England and Wales. The territories of Scotland, Northern Ireland, the Isle of Man and the Channel Islands have separate systems.

The term '**common law**' came to be used to describe the laws and customs applied by the royal courts which emerged after the Norman Conquest (1066). These new laws progressively replaced local laws and customs applied in local courts. The term common law is used, in a narrower sense, for one of a number of distinct sources of law that exist within such a system.

Laws enacted by the Queen in Parliament are called **Acts of Parliament** or **statutes**. These, and delegated powers conferred by statute, have arguably come to matter more today than the decisions of the courts.

By the thirteenth century, the crown had effectively delegated its inherent power to dispense justice to the judges.

Categories of law

There are many categories of law within the English legal system. Most notably, there are:

common law
equity
statute law
civil law
criminal law
private law
public law

All of these categories seem specially designed to confuse the student of law. To help you along, please see the brief descriptions and explanations below.

Common law

The term 'common law' refers to those legal systems which have adopted the English legal system – that is, its system of courts and procedures. Examples of countries which operate common law jurisdictions include many of the former Commonwealth countries, Australia and the United States. In general terms, a common law system refers to a unitary, national legal system under the control of a central power. In the United Kingdom the central power is the monarch. This is denoted in the UK courts by the presence of the Coat of Arms, representing the 'monarch's peace', or authority.

Equity

Before 1066, no national legal system existed in Britain. A dual system existed, with two jurisdictions side by side. These were the common law, and equity. This dichotomy derived from the two sets of legal principles in existence at that time, and from the two main courts which dealt with them:

(a) the Court of Exchequer, which implemented equitable principles
(b) the Courts of Common Pleas and King's Bench, which dispensed the common law.

This duality was finally ended by the Judicature Acts of 1873–75. The result of this legislation was to end the division between these jurisdictions.

Statute law

'Statute law' means law created by Parliament. This will be discussed further in Chapter 2 in detail.

Civil law

Civil law is that which regulates the legal relationships between individuals. For example it covers business contracts, property and land, commercial activities, employment and probate (including wills and property).

Criminal law

This law relates to the conduct between the state and individuals. Criminal law is concerned with enforcing or prohibiting particular types of behaviour. In sociological terms, the criminal law is the mechanism by which the state seeks to impose control upon its citizens.

Private law

The legal relationships between individual citizens are categorised as private law. Civil law is a category of private law.

Public law

Public law concerns the relationship between the citizen and the state. This law involves the regulation of state power. Criminal law is an example of public law. Since the 1980s, however, public law largely refers to **constitutional and administrative law**. This concerns the regulation of government activities and seeks to prevent the abuse of power by those who wield state control, in other words the government of the day.

Rule of law

According to Dicey, the 'rule of law' is a key feature of any constitution (*The Law of the Constitution*, 1885). Dicey and others believed that where the rule of law existed constitutionally, the exercise of arbitrary power by a state was impossible. Dicey therefore suggested that the rule of law had three distinct principles:

(a) there should be no abuse of power
(b) there should be equality before the law
(c) the law was supreme

Clearly, Dicey's version of the rule of law is outdated. However, the rule of law does have an important role in both our society and system of government. In particular, it requires all citizens to comply with law, be they monarch, politician, judge or ordinary citizen. The rule of law is meant to ensure that all can have recourse to the law, as well as to enforce the supremacy of the law.

Separation of powers
The doctrine of the separation of powers stems from the idea that government has three distinct functions:

1. legislative
2. executive
3. judicial

The **legislative** power refers to government's law-making powers, the drafting and passing of Acts of Parliament.

The **judicial** role of government refers to the judges and the courts system. This latter institution of modern government protects judicial independence. Judicial independence is essentially a principle by which the courts can hold government to account, and make it justify the exercise of its powers.

The **executive** denotes government and the huge departments of state it controls. The government is formed after a general election by the party which has most seats in the House of Commons. Moreover, it is believed that independence underpins these functions, due to the very nature of their separation. Thus we have the theory that the separation of powers prevents government exerting excessive power over its citizens. More simply, the separation of powers is about checking the powers of the major institutions of modern government. See figure 1 below for a brief illustration of such checks and balances at work.

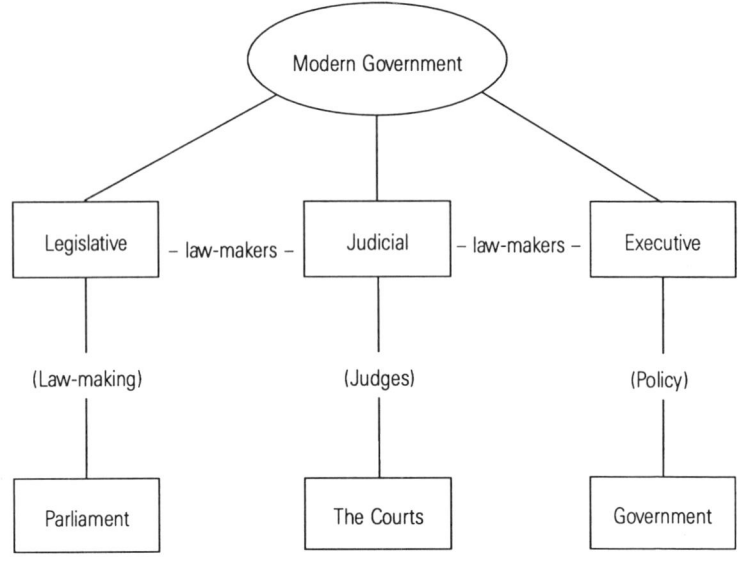

Fig. 1. The doctrine of the separation of powers.

Theories of law

Jurisprudence, the so-called philosophy of law, presents many theories on the nature of law. Each of theories categorises the purpose of law. The choice between law as a philosophy or a science is no doubt largely a matter of language. Modern day jurisprudence can be generally divided into three distinct groupings:

(a) the classical jurists (Austin and Bentham)
(b) the contemporary group (Hart and Dworkin)
(c) the critical grouping (Gramsci and Unger)

The classical jurists
John Austin and Jeremy Bentham epitomised the classical school of jurisprudence. These are often known as the 'black letter

lawyers'. That is, they believed in a body of rules, or laws, which make up a national system. This group of theories of law notes that law is made by an independently, democratic political process and law is used to express the wishes of the government of the day.

The contemporary group

The contemporary legal theorists, notably H L A Hart and Ronald Dworkin – also known as positivists – sought to critique the classical school, as set out above.

Hart, in particular, decided to turn his back on Austin and others. They believed that definitions resolved the difficulties in understanding relevant legal concepts. For Hart, the English legal system is a system of social rules. The law is a set of social rules because the law regulates society's behaviour, and so legal rules are derived from human behaviour.

Dworkin further refines Hart's theory of law. He analyses how judges should apply the law that other institutions have made, as well as make new law. On occasions this means that the judges must act as a deputy legislative body. Such a theory, of course, challenges the traditional form of the separation of powers. Dworkin brings into his theoretical perspective the dimension of 'rights', and the rights dialogue contained in law. Law is therefore seen as essentially political, as a lawmaker and an interpreter of social policy.

The critical school

The idea of 'critical legal studies' has grown tremendously over the last decade. This school of legal theory derives from a US movement in the late 1970s. It is a sceptical theory, as the use of the word 'critical' suggests. Critical legal thinkers such as Gramsci, Habermas and Unger believe that there is no distinctive mode of legal reasoning. Therefore, a critical legal perspective would be that law is a matter of politics. Critical legal theory centrally argues that law is concerned crucially with protecting freedom.

Legal theory covers a vast area and involves many different theories. Furthermore, the main three groupings listed above can be subdivided into many more specific theoretical groupings.

The law library

Both students of law, teachers of law, law practitioners and judges have one thing in common: they spend a large part of their lives in a law library. To all concerned with law, the law library and the law librarian are one of their most valuable resources.

Law libraries are commonly catalogued under five main areas:

(a) the statutes section
(b) the law reports
(c) journals and periodicals
(d) textbooks, monographs, bibliographic works and encyclopaedias
(e) electronic facilities

Textbooks are often arranged by subject, whereas journals and periodicals – as in most other libraries – are catalogued alphabetically. Law reports are displayed in date order and in various series of reports. These are often arranged alphabetically, too.

Dictionaries (such as Jowitts, Osborn's and the Concise Oxford) are very useful reference tools. So too are encyclopaedic works. The most notable of these is *Halsbury's Laws of England*, a most useful starting place for quick reference and research purposes. *Current Law* is another useful reference resource. This consists of weekly, monthly, annual and statutes series.

A law library can seem rather overwhelming. However, it will soon become a familiar workplace, once you have got an idea of the layout. All law programmes' induction weeks include a tour of the library and a chance to meet the law librarian

Only one further frustration exists – how to use a law report...

Reading law reports

All law students will find themselves spending many hours in the law library seeking out the endless references and case citations they meet in their studies. Finding and using law reports will soon become an everyday skill.

Since 1865 the body responsible for cataloguing law reports in the UK has been the **Incorporated Council of Law Reporting**. Before 1865 you would need to read case notes. Law reports were seldom published, and when they were they were they were in yearbook format, though some societies did in fact publish their own law reports (for example the Selden Society). Since 1865 there have evolved sets of law reports relating largely to the courts in which the cases reported were in fact heard.

However, today there exists a series of law reports commonly used by students and practitioners alike. The most common of these are:

(a) the weekly law reports (referred to as **WLR**)
(b) the All England Law Reports (**ALL ER**)
(c) European Court Reports/Common Market Law Reports (**ECR** and **CMLR**, reports of European law cases)
(d) Appeal Cases (cited as **AC**)

Other specialist law reports also exist. For example the weekly journal *Estates Gazette* (for property cases), the Industrial Relations Law Reports (more commonly known as **IRLR**), the family law reports (referred to as **FLR**), and so on.

Example
To find a law report, the following quick step-by-step guide might be useful for the novice. See the example citation below:

Hardy v. Salford University [1998] 1 SHLR 204

The example citation explained:

Hardy v. Salford University–[1998]–1–SHLR–204

(Parties' names)–(year case held)–(volume of report)–(name of law report)–(page number).

Here are some more examples:

Example 1
Donoghue v. Stevenson [1932] AC 562

D (the plaintiff/appellant) & S (the defendant/respondent) are the litigants. This case is reported in the Appeal Cases reports for 1932, commencing at p.562.

Example 2
Costa v. ENEL [1964] ECR 585
C (the plaintiff) & ENEL (the respondent) are the litigants. This case is reported in the European Court reports for 1964, commencing at p.585.

Example 3
DPP v. Blake [1989] 1 WLR 432
DPP (the plaintiff/appellant) & B (the defendant/respondent) are the litigants. This case is reported in the Weekly Law Reports for 1989, starting on page 432.

Example 4
R. v. Reading Crown Court, ex p Bello [1992] 3 All ER 353
R (the Crown) (the appellant) & Bello (the ex parte respondent) (a matter about an appeal from a decision of Reading Crown Court) (are the litigants). This case is reported in Volume 3 of the All England Law Reports for 1992 starting on page 353.

Now look up these law reports in your local law library. Try some other examples for yourself. You will find it will help to consult a legal dictionary and make yourself a list all the law reports abbreviations for future use.

Legal skills

Teaching and learning methods
The English legal system, and law more generally, is taught in many different ways. The traditional way means lectures and seminar/tutorials. However, in more recent times open, distance and electronic learning have created new ways of learning about the law. Even so, the following remain the most common methods of teaching law:

1. case method – a US teaching style in which a case study and materials are used to illustrate legal principles at work

2. the Socratic method – students recite the details of cases and explain their legal significance to their peers in class

3. clinical legal education – students are engaged part-time or on a placement to a law firm

4. mooting/mock trials – the law students role-play, and present oral legal argument as if in court

Building your skills base

Amongst all this learning of the law we need to keep in mind the development of skills. Historically, legal education has been rigidly divided into academic legal education and vocational training. Both share a desire to build the student's skill base. These skills include:

(a) *reasoning skills* – the ability to present a clearly written legal argument

(b) *advocacy skills* – presenting an oral coherently structured and argued case

(c) *analytical skills* – comprehension, assessment and evaluation, in other words being able to consider facts and apply the relevant law and advise persons on their rights and liabilities

(d) *interviewing skills* – being able to extract from people relevant, accurate and reliable information. This includes the ability to listen and counsel people. Good interpersonal skills are involved here

(e) *drafting skills* – constructing simple statements of complex issues, and presenting clearly written legal argument

(f) *negotiating skills* – many tutors, like the author of this Studymate, hope that this skill is not only exercised by the student wanting to negotiate a deadline extension for their forthcoming assignment, but more productively in the way they plan and share their studies with other students, staff and others

(g) *IT skills* – attaining competent information technology and computer literacy skills

These seven core skills provide a foundation upon which the student can build confidence and competence in their learning of law.

Often students are unaware of how far they are gaining these valuable skills. To make sure you do not fall into this trap, see the legal skills chart in the Appendix. When doing lecture, seminar or tutorial preparation and assignments, mark off your activities against the checklist provided. Some students may wish to draft an action plan for themselves so they can monitor and measure their own progress.

Note-taking

A vital everyday skill of the typical law student is note-taking. Lectures, seminars, tutorials and researching are the core means by which a law student acquires knowledge, and so her/his ability to take accurate, reliable and readable notes is essential. For some students note-taking is easy and comes naturally. Others find it a struggle. Whatever your own level of competence, making a verbatim transcript does not represent good note-taking, nor is it an effective way of learning. As both a student, and as a tutor, I have watched many students taking advantage of modern technology and tape-recording lecturers, seminars/tutorials and so on. But this is only a fruitful exercise if put to good use by the student after the lecture, and a set of notes taken. Good note-taking is an art and one which is gained by practice.

To that end, here are some note-taking tips drawn from many years' experience first as a student and now as a tutor:

▶ *Knowledge* – Notes provide a body of material. That material is knowledge. That knowledge assists you in an examination or any other assessment.

▶ *Collation* – Keep all of your notes together, maybe in a file. For law as a discipline, it is important that you group your notes by subjects studied (for example tort, contract, criminal, constitutional, EC, property, trusts).

▶ *Layout* – Find a way of setting out your notes. For example you could leave a large blank column down the right hand side of a page, so you have space to add notes later, or to amend them should the law change or a landmark case appear in the course of your studies. These things always happen!

▶ *Notation of cases* – Always underline the names of cases. (Be sure to obtain and write down the correct citation – this will be crucial later....) This is very much a convention for law-writing, especially in assignments.

▶ *Abbreviations* – Develop your own system of abbreviations. Headings and sub-headings are always useful (these particularly aid revision later in your studies).

▶ *Avoid repetition* – To do this you must be selective. Try to cultivate a way of listening (in lectures) and a way of reading (when in the library) that will help you identify peripheral material. This skill will not come easily at first, but with practice and experience it will grow. Once familiar with the terminology and subject, you will develop a keen law editor's eye for relevancy. A good example of this skill at work is when you come to analyse case law (see Chapters 2 and 3 for further details). Your ability to locate the head note and to extrapolate the *ratio decidendi* will be crucial to your studies and your learning.

▶ *Examples* – Always use examples to illustrate your points (especially case law examples, if applicable) to aid your understanding later.

▶ *Answering questions* – If questions are posed, do make sure that you always answer them clearly and definitively.

To some readers, the foregoing will seem obvious. Others may well find that these techniques will significantly improve their learning. As already suggested, note-taking is an art, and personal to each and everyone of us.

Have the courage to ask

Above all the student of law must overcome their greatest fear and have the courage to ask questions. The competent law student will always ask pertinent questions. He or she does not have to know all the answers. It was once said that, 'It was only a foolish lawyer who represented himself.' In the same way, it would be a foolish student who believed they had all the answers.

Seek advice and assistance from your tutor. It is an important part of their job to provide it! The best way of getting all your questions answered is to prepare thoroughly for your seminars/ tutorials and list any queries you may have. Then put them to the tutor at your seminar or tutorial, or at a convenient time afterwards. Effective seminars have three key ingredients:

(a) good preparation
(b) a contribution by the student(s) to discussion and debate
(c) making use of the tutor

Good planning and organising (researching)

Another common pitfall for the student of law is failing to plan and organise their time. Students of law may find it useful to timetable their studies beyond their classroom contact time. This may indeed be essential if they want to access the internet and other electronic resources. Law students should plan their time carefully, in order to take advantage of all the possible resources – tutors, the library, computing facilities, mooting event, other electronic information systems such as LEXIS, Smith Bernal Case Law, Lawtel, and others – as well as budgeting time for all important social activities and family commitments.

For further details on preparing your work and working towards assessment, see the Appendix. Remember, your academic studies will not only equip you with knowledge, but more often than not with increased competence in some of the skills listed above. For readers hoping to embark upon careers in the legal profession, or related professions, these skills will prove of immense benefit to you in both your vocational courses and in the workplace. In the meantime, they may help you win a place on a vocational course, or in employment.

The acquisition of skills should never be underestimated as a useful study resource. Nowadays, many law courses (if not all) in the UK are designed to help their students acquire these skills, even if not formally structured into their various law programmes.

Tutorial

Practice questions
The following questions will help you revise and learn how to study the law effectively:

1. Write down short definitions for each of the following legal labels: common law, equity, public law, and criminal law. Give an example of each.

2. What is the doctrine of separation of powers?

3. Describe the principle of the rule of law. What does this rule mean for the English legal system?

4. Outline each of the main theories of law.

If you are not sure how to answer any of these questions, then spend a few minutes reading this chapter again.

Seminar discussion
'Law is a result of philosophy and not science.' How far would you agree with this statement, bearing in mind the various theories of law?

Student assignment
Set aside some time to plan and set up a really effective note-taking strategy and information management system.

Further reading
Lloyd & Freeman, *Lloyd's Introduction to Jurisprudence* (5 ed.), 1985, Stevens.
Slapper & Kelly, *English Legal System* (3 ed.), 1997, Cavendish.
Kenny, *Studying Law* (3 ed.), 1994, Butterworths.

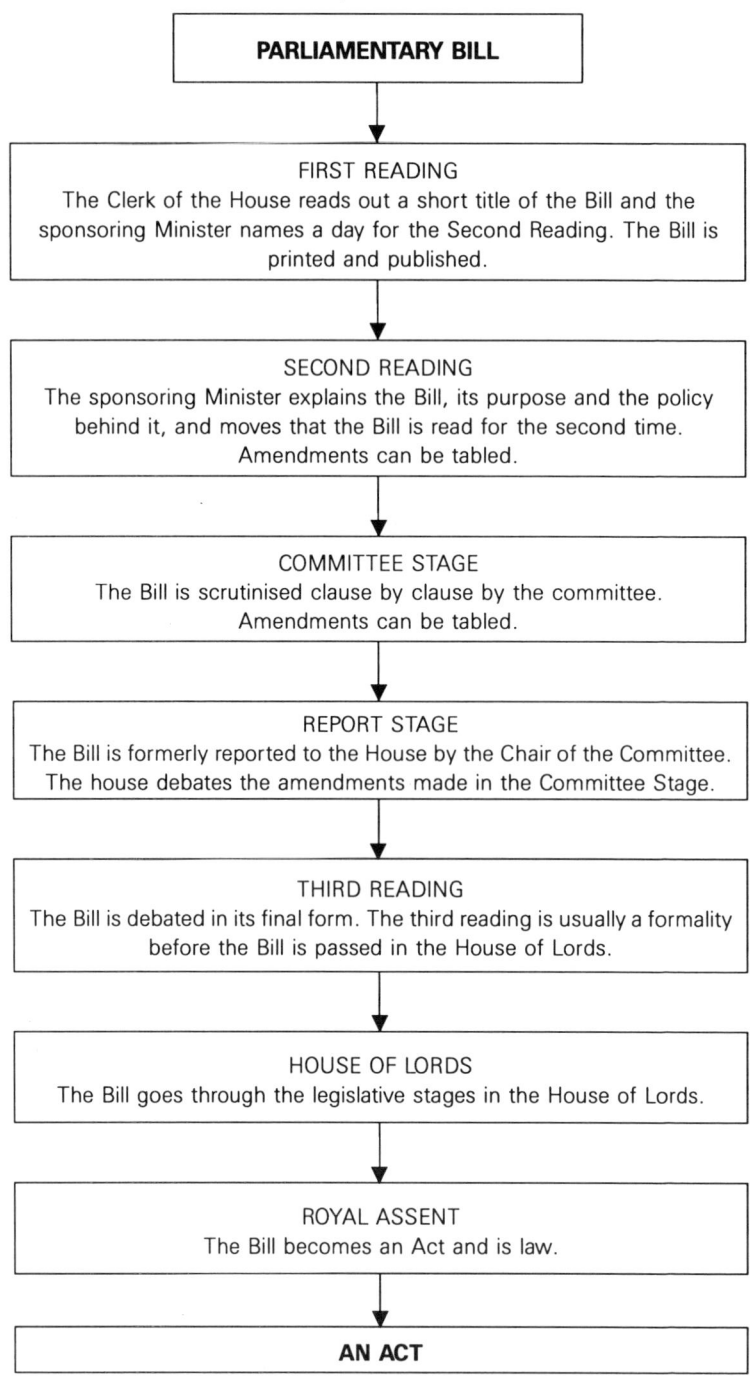

PARLIAMENTARY BILL

FIRST READING
The Clerk of the House reads out a short title of the Bill and the sponsoring Minister names a day for the Second Reading. The Bill is printed and published.

SECOND READING
The sponsoring Minister explains the Bill, its purpose and the policy behind it, and moves that the Bill is read for the second time. Amendments can be tabled.

COMMITTEE STAGE
The Bill is scrutinised clause by clause by the committee. Amendments can be tabled.

REPORT STAGE
The Bill is formerly reported to the House by the Chair of the Committee. The house debates the amendments made in the Committee Stage.

THIRD READING
The Bill is debated in its final form. The third reading is usually a formality before the Bill is passed in the House of Lords.

HOUSE OF LORDS
The Bill goes through the legislative stages in the House of Lords.

ROYAL ASSENT
The Bill becomes an Act and is law.

AN ACT

Fig. 2. The legislative process.

2

Understanding the Sources of Law

One minute summary – This chapter examines how the law is made in the UK. It will outline the parliamentary legislative processes and the impact of the courts upon the common law. In this chapter you will learn about the:

▶ law-making processes in the UK
▶ legal significance of parliament
▶ role of custom in law
▶ rules of precedent
▶ impact of European and international law on the English legal tradition

Law-making in the UK

The British constitutional settlement following the Bill of Rights of 1688 gave sovereignty to parliament to make law. 'Sovereignty' loosely means the power to make and unmake laws. In modern day language this means that the elected parliament at Westminster has the power to enact and repeal Acts of parliament. The British government of the day is formed by the party which wins the largest number of seats in the House of Commons, that is the one with the highest number of members of parliament returned after a general election. It has a democratic mandate and can pass the laws it sees fit to pass, or has promised to pass, in its election manifesto.

The process for passing Acts of parliament – Bills as they are called before they reach the statute book – is rooted in medieval tradition. The process involves a course of debates, known as readings, followed by scrutiny by a committee, then a vote and the Queen's assent, as set out in figure 2:

The parliamentary legislative process

▶ *First reading.* Here the Bill, that is the proposed legislation, is introduced and a date and time is announced when its first debate will take place.

▶ *Second reading.* At this stage the Bill is debated. The views of MPs and the political parties are expressed.

▶ *Committee stage.* Following a second reading, the Bill is sent to the appropriate Select Committee (departmental) or Standing Committee (special ones set up for particular issues on an ad hoc basis). There, evidence is taken from experts on the issue and from the civil servants and ministers responsible. In Committee the proposed Bill is scrutinised in detail. Also, at this stage amendments can be tabled and voted upon, in order to modify the Bill.

▶ *Report stage.* Following the requisite Committee's hearings, the MPs who make up the Committee draft and produce a report, which is tabled to the House in which the legislation began.

▶ *Third reading.* At last the Bill and the proposed ('tabled') amendments are debated and voted upon in the House.

▶ *Other House/final vote.* Each Bill then goes to the other House (Commons or Lords) to repeat the above-mentioned procedure, before returning to its original House for a final vote.

▶ *Royal assent.* Having been passed by both Houses of Parliament, every Bill is then sent to the monarch for royal assent. Whilst constitutionally this has become a customary formality of rubber stamping, in fact the monarch still has the power to withhold her consent to a Bill. Once approved, the Bill becomes an Act.

Parliament

Parliament is bicameral, that is it is comprised of two chambers or Houses. These are the House of Commons, and the House of Lords (or peers). The House of Commons is composed of 681 elected Members of Parliament (MPs). These divide to make up the:

1. government, including the prime minister and other ministers of state, and

2. opposition, which includes the official leader of the opposition and shadow spokespersons (these are the minister's counterpart in opposition) and the other opposition parties and their leaders.

In contrast, the House of Lords at present consists of unelected peers, most of whom are hereditary. The hereditary peers are entitled to sit in the Lords by right of birth, as offspring of a noble family – dukes, marquesses, earls, viscounts and barons – or are members of the Royal family.

The other members of the House of Lords are life peers, given the right to sit in the upper chamber until their death. The latter group is largely made up of former politicians or senior public figures, such as leaders of industry or the trade unions. Also in the Lords are the archbishops (of York and Canterbury), 26 bishops of the Church of England, and the **law lords**. The latter are the most senior judges in the UK and comprise the highest court within the UK jurisdiction. This will be discussed in detail below in chapter 7.

In the absence of the monarch, the Lord Chancellor chairs the business in the House of Lords. By tradition he sits on the woolsack which is positioned in front of the throne. In the House of Commons the debates are governed by the Speaker, who is the Queen's official representative in the Commons. The Lord Chancellor is appointed by the government, and he is a member of the cabinet as well as being the most senior judge and highest judicial office holder in the UK. The Speaker is elected by the Commons on a rota basis, and the Speakership alternates between the government and opposition for tenures of office. Please note that reform of the composition of the House of Lords is currently under discussion. (see http://www.lords-reform.org.uk).

Bills

Both Houses of Parliament play a part in the legislative process. Normally, this process begins in the House of Commons, but legislation can be initiated in the House of Lords. This usually depends upon the type of Bill concerned. Generally, there are three types of Bill. They are a:

1. *Public Bill* – one normally presented, if not supported, by the government.

2. *Private Bill* – as the title suggests, one which deals with something which may not be a matter of huge public concern, but which still requires enactment by parliament. For example, it may be required for the building of a road, or any other large public planning project, or the granting of a licence. Private Bills like these are usually started in the House of Lords.

3. *Private Member's Bill* – These are Bills presented by individual MPs on issues where they wish to amend the law. They are often derived from pressure groups. For example, the Abortion Act of 1967 began life as a Private Member's Bill, sponsored by the then Sir David Steel MP (now Lord Steel).

Law made by the courts

Aside from being enacted by legislation, law is also made by the courts within the UK. Law made in this way is known as the **common law**, or **case law**. Although the courts cannot challenge Acts of Parliament, they can and do often have to interpret their meaning and enforce the ensuing judgments. This will be explored throughout this text, and the courts and the role of the judiciary will be discussed in some detail later in Chapter 3.

Primary and secondary legislation

Returning briefly to legislation, UK statutes or Acts of Parliament are subdivided into two types:

▶ **Primary legislation** – This refers to Acts of Parliament, as enacted by the parliamentary legislative process described above.

▶ **Secondary (delegated) legislation** – This is legislation made by a Minister, the Secretary of State responsible, or his civil servants (acting in *alter ego*), using powers to draft and enact given to the Minister by a particular Act of Parliament. The term 'delegated' best defines the process: a delegation from the Act to the Minister responsible to make law as she or he sees fit. Secondary or delegated legislation is normally referred to by lawyers as **statutory instrument(s)**. Of these statutory instruments, the Minister can decide whether they shall be enacted as Regulations (the most common form), Rules, Circulars, Codes of Practice, or Guidance.

Even though a Minister has the power under various Acts of Parliament (primary legislation) to enact statutory instruments, this delegated legislation still has to be published and persons affected must be consulted.

Also, it still has to be placed before parliament, subject to various procedures for discussion (for example, the prayer of annulment procedure), before it can become law. The Statutory Instruments Act 1946 makes this extra-parliamentary process very clear. The aim is to deter Ministers from passing hostile legislation quickly and without public knowledge. In the context of modern government, Circulars, Codes of Practice and Guidance are the most influential statutory instruments and widely control the functioning of local government and other governmental service providers. Due to the enormous structure of British government and the complexity of society, the use of statutory instruments as a means of law-making has become more and more common.

Custom and practice

Custom and practice have a bearing on law. Elaborated, clarified and defined, long-established custom and practice can become law, even though they have not been embodied in parliamentary legislation. Over the years, legal institutions have taken established practice and evolved it to reflect the needs of modern society. A good example is today's mercantile law which has its roots in the practice of merchants in the fourteenth century. The law therefore does, in part, recognise custom.

However, in order for custom to become law it must be generally recognised that the custom has existed for a long period of time –

since 'time immemorial'. It must have been exercised throughout that period of time and been accepted without opposition. It happens rarely, but the courts so sometimes rely upon custom as the source of law where they see it appropriate to do. The latest example of the courts exercising this discretionary right was in a case in Yorkshire where a hawthorn bush was preserved and a planning order quashed. It was shown to be customary practice in that locality to preserve old hawthorn bushes.

Case law

Case law means the law determined and refined by the courts. The structure of the courts in the UK is hierarchical, and so the higher the court the more influential and binding its decision ill be upon the community at large. The House of Lords stands at the summit of the English legal system, and so its decisions are binding on all the courts below. In fact, until 1966 the House of Lords was bound by its own previous decisions. In case law, the principle of *stare decisis* – binding precedent as it is more commonly known – refers to the English legal concept in which the lower courts are bound by the decisions of the higher courts.

Binding precedent?

When considering precedent, students of law often ask: Does 'precedent' mean that all of the court's decision is binding? The short answer is no. A court's decision is made up of many parts. However, there are two essential parts:

1. the **ratio decidendi** – This is the rule of law on which the decision is made from the facts of the given case. The *ratio decidendi* is therefore the statement of the law applied in determining the legal problem raised in the case under judicial scrutiny: in other words the reasons behind the decision.

2. **obiter dictum** – This refers to the superfluous part of the legal judgement which is how the decision was reached and not a point of law.

EU, international and UK law?

The influence of both European and international law as a source of English law should not be underestimated. European law, including human rights law, will be examined in detail in Chapter 7.

International law has assisted in vigorously reforming English law. Consider for example the impact of the United Nations Charter of Fundamental Human Rights, and of other international documents such as the Vienna Convention on Diplomatic Rights, the International Law of the Sea, and the UN Convention on the Rights of the Child. However, international law only has an impact in English law where:

(a) the UK is a signatory, and
(b) the current domestic law is ambiguous and requires clarification

Law reform

Law is constantly changing. Under English law there are three methods of bringing about law reform:

1. **Royal Commissions** – These are an *ad hoc* mechanism, constituted by government, for the purpose of informing reform

2. **Green and White Papers** – These are another government apparatus for measuring the opinions of those affected or likely to be affected by a proposed reform.

3. **Law Commission** – This is a permanent, independent advisory body whose function is to review the current law and make recommendations.

Tutorial

Practice questions
The following questions will help you revise and understand the sources of law:

1. Write down a list of all the main sources of English law.

2. What is the significance of parliamentary sovereignty to the sources of English law? Summarise the parliamentary law-making process, and explain each stage in detail.

3. Explain the principle of binding precedent.

4. What do the expressions *ratio decidendi* and *obiter dictum* mean?

If you are not sure how to answer any of these questions, then spend a few minutes reading this chapter again.

Seminar discussion
Can law be changed? Discuss this issue in view of the various mechanisms for law reform.

Further reading
Ingham, *The English Legal Process*, 1996, Blackstone Press.
Slapper & Kelly, *English Legal System* (3 ed.), 1997, Cavendish.

3

The Judges and the Law

One minute summary – In this chapter you will explore the mechanisms of judicial reasoning, the so-called rules of statutory interpretation and precedent. You will learn what statutory interpretation is and how it works, what the principle rules are, and the role of the English judge as an interpreter. The chapter covers:

- ▶ introduction
- ▶ statutory interpretation
- ▶ binding precedent
- ▶ the judge as legal interpreter

Introduction

As you already know, primary legislation is created by parliament. Drafting, the so-called preparation of statutes, is undertaken by civil servants known as parliamentary counsel. These civil servants are responsible for translating political objectives, often contained in political parties' manifestoes, into draft legal form. In other words, their task is to turn policy proposals into law. According to Francis Bennion (1978), a well-known legal scholar and former parliamentary counsel, the criteria for translating political initiatives into legislation are:

(a) certainty
(b) legal effectiveness
(c) procedural legitimacy
(d) timeliness
(e) comprehensibility
(f) acceptability

(g) brevity
(h) debatability
(i) legal compatibility

Bennion believed that such criteria helped parliament in its legislative work as the primary law-maker and the passing of Bills into Acts, as discussed in the earlier chapters of this text. However, the flood of proposed new legislation after the end of the second world war (1939–45) meant that another mechanism was needed to enable laws to be made. As a result, delegated legislation – statutory instruments as they are more commonly termed – emerged (see the Statutory Instruments Act 1946). Alongside these legal developments arose a new judicial duty, that of **statutory interpretation**. We will now explore what statutory interpretation is.

Statutory interpretation

According to the celebrated writer George Bernard Shaw (author of *Man and Superman*), 'The golden rule is that there are no golden rules.' However, against such advice the British legal system has created and endorsed over centuries some principal rules of statutory interpretation, and the judges follow these rules when dealing with cases. Whilst set within boundaries, however, judicial reasoning as we shall see is often a law unto itself. However, the primary constitutional role of the judge is to *apply* the law, since it is the role of parliament to *create* the law in the first place.

The rules of statutory interpretation

Three principal rules of statutory interpretation exist, as follows:

▶ *The Literal Rule* – This means that the judge should give words in legislation their literal meaning, that is their everyday meaning.

▶ *The Golden (or Purposive) Rule* – Generally, this rule extends the literal rule, by applying the literal interpretation to the circumstances and seek the purpose of the rule and reach a proper conclusion against an absurdity which a literal interpretation might bring. For an example of the Golden Rule in action, see River Wear Commissioners v Adamson [1876 – 77] 2 App Cas 743 at 764–5, per Lord Blackburn's speech.

▶ *The Mischief Rule* -This rule embodies the most flexible approach to the interpretation of legislation. Most simply, it seeks to allow judges to go beyond the strict meaning of the legislation. Its origins are in the Heydon's Case [1584] 3 Co Rep 7a. This says that when interpreting legislation, 'mischievous' judges should consider the common law prior to the Act. They should discover why the Act was enacted and what problem it was seeking to remedy; and why parliament sought the remedy shown in the Act. Consequently, judges are permitted to seek justifiable exceptions to the rules based on common sense and/or the need to dispense justice to the parties concerned.

The canons of construction
In addition to the rules of statutory interpretation, further help can be had by consulting various canons of construction, as set out below:

▶ *Title of the Act* – A title of an Act should itself provide a general intention of what the Act is seeking to achieve. Often an Act will have a preamble which will also state the main purpose of the legislation. Such intentions will be very helpful to judges when deciding cases. For example, the Interpretation Act 1978 is a valuable source of assistance when seeking to define various legal terms. For example, see R v. Glavin [1987] QB 862.

▶ *Words and lists* – Lists of words, or just a repetition of a well-understood word, can also help judges to interpret a statute, as in Coltman v Bibby Dancers [1988] AC 276 HL.

▶ *Interpretation Act 1978* – The Interpretation Act 1978 was enacted to define common legal terms. For example a 'month' means calendar month and not 30 days.

▶ *Punctuation* – Following the case of Dixon v BBC [1979] 2 All ER 112, it is clear that the basic tenets of English grammar and punctuation, which give emphasis to certain words in various contexts, should help judges in their interpretation of legislation.

▶ *Dictionaries* – Clearly, dictionaries, legal, medical or otherwise, are indeed another useful source of reference for interpretation. See Flack v Baldry [1988] 1 WLR 393 for confirmation of this.

▶ *Travaux preparatoires* – Most Acts result from reports from various institutions, either Parliamentary, the Law Commission or other lobbying groups, and as a consequence these reports are very useful when seeking to interpret legislation. Therefore, Law Commission working papers and Hansard, particularly since Pepper v Hart [1992] 3 WLR 1032 HL (See Evans & Slapper [1993] *Journal of Business Law*, March, at p.185, for further commentary), where a Minister's words used when introducing legislation can be used as guidance as to its meaning.

▶ *Other statutes* – Other statutes can sometimes be useful for interpretation. This applies especially to those *in pari materia,* which means 'concerning the same matter'. This often applies when judges have to interpret European Community laws.

▶ *Ejusdem generis* – The *ejusdem generis* principle is one of the presumptions allowed under the general rules of interpretation by the courts. This presumption applies where general words are specifically listed at the end of a statute. For instance, 'domestic animals means cats and dogs'. For example, see Brown Sea Haven Properties Ltd v Poole Corp [1958] 1 All ER 205.

▶ *Noscitur a sociis* – This is another presumptive principle applied where an Act lists examples of what is covered by the legislation. For further elaboration, see Foster v Diphwys Callan Slate Co [1887] 18 QBD 428.

► *Expressio unius exclusio alterius* – The final presumption is this one which means that anything not included in the Act is therefore expressly excluded. See, for example, R v Cuthbertson [1980] 2 All ER 401.

Binding precedent

Consistency is seen as a hallmark of legal reasoning, so the doctrine of precedent is viewed as an acceptable feature of the English legal system. As a result, the decisions of the superior courts of the United Kingdom can bind the decisions of the lower courts. Such **binding precedent** has become known as *stare decisis*, which means 'keep to what has been decided previously'.

Due to this rule of binding precedent judges are bound by the judgements of their counterparts in the higher courts. This does not, of course, apply to the law lords who sit in the highest court, House of Lords. This rule was established as long ago as 1898. (It was changed in 1966 to enable the Court of Appeal to also not be bound by previous decisions of the House of Lords.) So today, from the Court of Appeal upwards, the judges can interpret law as they think fit, unbound by what they have previously decided.

The judge as legal interpreter

In Cardoza (1921) were uttered the famous US judge's words: 'The judicial process was not one to discover, but creation'. Often the line between law and fact is both a difficult and blurred one. When such situations as these arise, the judge and/or the jury are asked to find the *ratio decidendi* – 'the reason for deciding'. This reason can be any rule of law which may guide them in reaching a decision.

Where such an activity is at work, a judge may decide may decide to adopt more that one *ratio*. In fact, where two or more *ratio* exists then one or more is deemed not necessary for the court's conclusion and is deemed *obiter dictum*. That which is not deemed *obiter dictum* is the correct proposition of law upon which the judge's decision rests.

Tutorial

Practice questions
The following questions will help you revise and understand the role of the judges as statutory interpreters of the law:

1. What principal rules of statutory interpretation exist in English law? Explain and provide an example for each rule.

2. Discuss the contribution of the so-called canons of construction made to the interpretation of legislation.

3. 'Ministers ought to be careful of what they say in parliament today, since they may live to regret it in court.' (Lord Chancellor, Lord Mackay of Clashfern). Evaluate this statement in light of the House of Lords ruling in Pepper v. Hart (1992) 3 WLR 1032.

4. Identify the principal rules of statutory interpretation.

5. Summarise what the 'Golden', 'Literal' and 'Mischief' rules mean.

6. Explain the meaning and operation of the 'canons of construction'.

7. Explain the role of the judge as an interpreter.

If you are not sure how to answer any of these questions, then spend a few minutes reading this chapter again.

Seminar discussion
1. Do you consider the doctrine of binding precedent limits or empowers the role of judges as legal interpreters?

2. Has British membership of the European Union clarified or muddied the rules governing statutory interpretation?

Further reading
Holland and Webb, *Learning Legal Rules* (2ed.), 1995, Blackstone.
Twining and Miers, *How to Do Things with Rules* (3 ed.), 1991, Weidenfeld & Nicolson.
Zander, *The Law-Making Process* (4ed.), 1991, Butterworths.

4

The National Courts System

One minute summary – By the term 'UK' courts we mean those in England and Wales, Scotland and Northern Ireland. It is important to recognise that there are three separate legal systems when we consider courts structures: the Scottish, Northern Irish, and the English (the latter incorporating Wales). This chapter will explain both the formal and informal methods of law enforcement, and system of resolution of disputes in the UK. You will also learn to recognise and understand the functions of the various civil and criminal courts and tribunals. This chapter will cover:

▶ the three separate legal systems
▶ UK civil courts
▶ UK criminal courts
▶ civil courts reform and Lord Woolf
▶ the prison system

Three separate legal systems

The system in England and Wales
In England and Wales, since the Norman Conquest of 1066, the UK legal system and its courts have undergone radical reformation from Curia Regis, the King's courts, to ecclesiastical courts, to Common Pleas, to the Court of Chancery, to the reforms of the 1970s and 1980s, to the courts today. Divided between civil and criminal jurisdictions, the British courts system makes up a complex web of different rules, jurisdictions and judges. Figures 3 and 4 illustrate the current system:

The system in Scotland
Law in Scotland is governed by a separate legal regime of courts

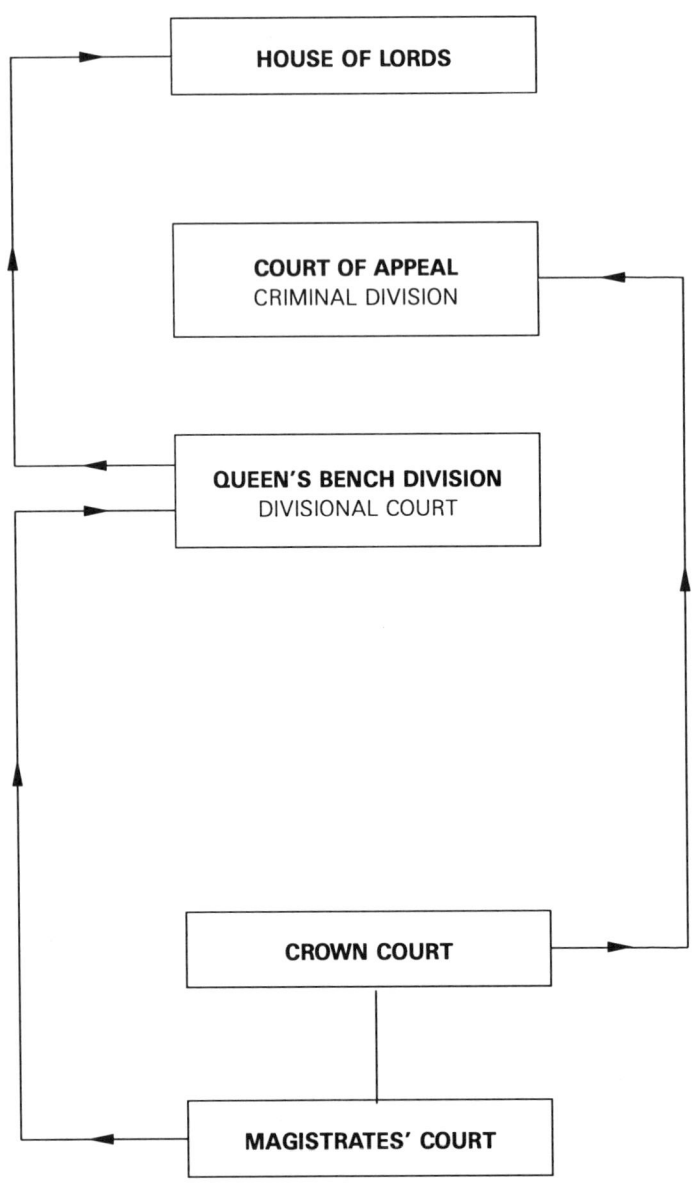

Fig. 3. The principal courts exercising criminal jurisdiction.

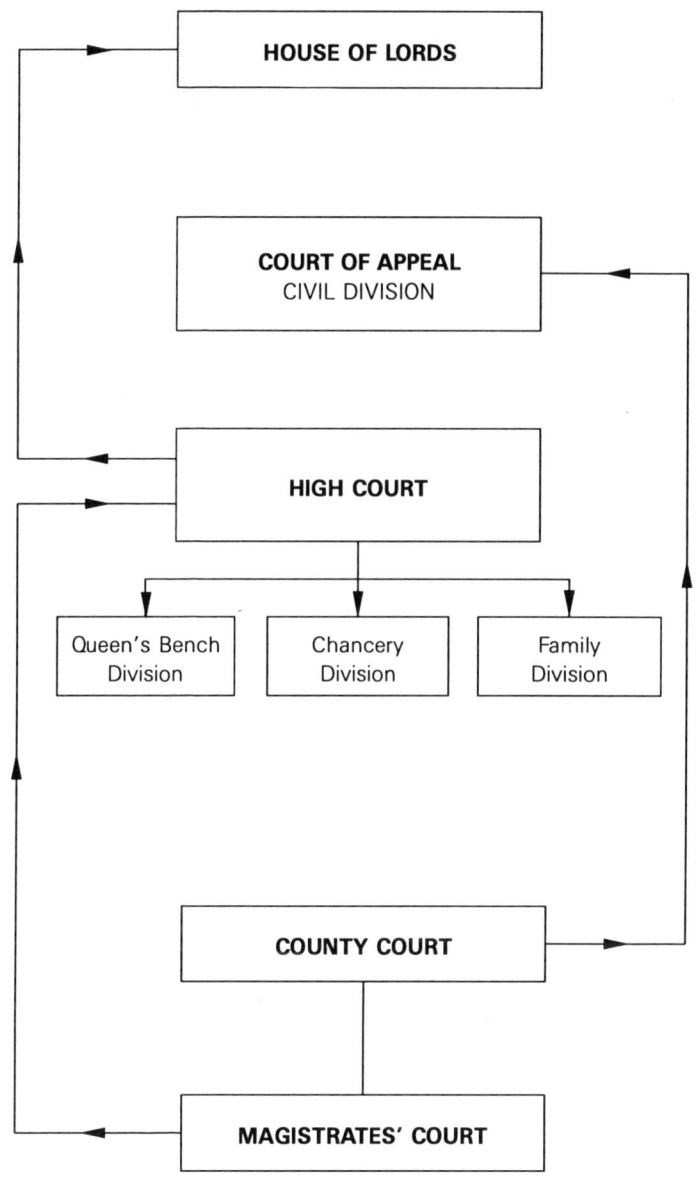

Fig. 4. The principal courts exercising civil jurisdiction.

and procedures. Much influenced by Roman law, the Scottish
legal system has a different courts structure. For example, in the
lowest level criminal courts, a district court or sheriff's court
replaces the English (and Welsh) magistrates' and crown courts.
As for civil matters, a sheriff's court replaces its Welsh/English
counterpart, the county court.

Scotland has its own appeal courts, the Court of Session in civil
matters, and the High Court of Justiciary in criminal proceedings.
However, any further appeals lie to the House of Lords. The
higher courts of Scotland are based in Edinburgh. Consequently,
the Scottish judiciary and legal profession are different from those
in the English/Welsh jurisdiction. The prosecutors are known as
'procurators'. As elsewhere, the rules of evidence remain complex
and technical. Under the Legal Aid (Scotland) Act 1986, the legal
provisions are almost identical to those in both England and
Wales. You should be aware that all these differences lead to
distinctions in certain legal provisions.

The system in Northern Ireland

In Northern Ireland, the courts system is the same as in England
and Wales, except that Northern Ireland has its own appeal court.
From here appeal once again lies to the House of Lords.
Irrespective of these departures from the English/Welsh legal
traditions, European Community law supersedes their respective
domestic laws, as it does in both England and Wales.

Civil and criminal law

Since the UK courts are divided into both civil and criminal
courts, the law too must be conveniently packaged in the same
manner. In view of this dichotomy let us explain here the
fundamental difference of these distinct paths, which governs the
whole process of British law:

(a) **Criminal law** is mainly concerned with disputes between the
State and individuals.

(b) **Civil law** governs the relationships between individuals in
society.

This historical distinction arose more by accident than by design. It has been a matter of tradition that recurring legal matters have been dealt with for centuries by particular courts. This division between criminal and civil law has survived centuries of legal reform. Let us now examine those individual courts in detail.

UK criminal courts

These are primarily concerned with the prosecution of persons for criminal offences.

Magistrates' courts

These are the inferior (lowest level) criminal courts. They are supervised by legally qualified clerks, and lay or stipendiary magistrates. Formerly described as 'petty sessional' courts, they deal with minor criminal offences, such as assaults, burglary and breach of the peace. They also handle committal proceedings, in which those accused of more serious offences are committed (sent) for trial to crown court.

A major part of the work of the magistrates courts is to operate as youth courts dealing with juveniles under the age of 18. Consequently, magistrates have separate sentencing guidelines and powers for dealing with juveniles. For these purposes, a national **Youth Justice Board** was established in 1998 to oversee the setting of guidelines for both the sentencing and treatment of young offenders. The youth court is less formal and sometimes sits in private, in order to protect accused youths from public exposure. In any event, magistrates can order that a young defendant's name is not reported in the press, although the facts of the crimes and the punishment can.

Appeals lie from the magistrates courts to the Crown court.

Crown courts

Lord Beeching's Commission in 1966 set up the assizes and quarter sessions courts. Under the Courts Act 1971 these became known as crown courts. In these courts, trial is by:

(a) judge – who deals with legal questions, and

(b) jury – made up of twelve lay persons who consider the facts and determine whether the defendant is guilty or not guilty.

These courts can be supervised by high court judges, but more often they are supervised by circuit judges or recorders or assistant recorders (part-time judges). They are organised into circuits, six in all in the UK. The crown courts deal with more serious criminal offences, such as murder, manslaughter, rape, serious assault, fraud, robbery and conspiracy. Appeals from the crown courts on points of law lie to the High Court.

Criminal Cases Review Commission

As a result of miscarriages of justice that came to light in the late 1980s and early 1990s, a Criminal Cases Review Commission was set up in April 1997. Based in Birmingham, its major task is to investigate any alleged miscarriages of justice. In taking over this responsibility from the Home Office, the Commission has wide powers to reopen police investigations and can order cases to be referred to the Crown Court and Court of Appeal.

The UK civil courts

These are concerned with the resolution of disputes between complainant parties.

Magistrates' courts

Despite having a primarily criminal jurisdiction, magistrates' courts also have a civil remit. In particular, they have an extensive role in family and child law. They have power to make financial orders, and orders to protect the welfare of children. Consequently, the magistrates' court has a separate family court. Magistrates also have civil duties such as enforcing the payment of rates, enforcing the collection of taxes, licensing of premises for entertainment and the sale of alcohol, and gaming registration.

In civil matters, appeal lies from a magistrates' court to the county or High Court.

County courts

County courts were set up under the County Courts Act 1846. The UK has been divided into districts, making up various local registries for dealing with civil disputes. There are more than 260 county courts in the UK. Cases are heard by a district or circuit judge, depending upon their nature and jurisdiction. The disputes heard range from contractual matters, to land disputes, probate and family matters, and admiralty claims. Claims of less than £50,000 are heard in county courts. Claims of less than £3,000 are classified as small claims, and for these there is a special procedure where costs are not awarded against the loser. Appeals on civil matters over the value of £50,000 are heard in the High Court. Since 26 April 1999 and the effect of the 'Woolf Reforms', seeking to eliminate unnecessary cost; minimise delay; and reduce complexity, the Civil Procedure Act 1997 provides from 3 types of civil claim: (a) small claims (less than £5,000), (b) fast track claims (below £15,000), (c) claims over £15,000.

The High Court

Not peculiar to the UK system, but very distinct from other jurisdictions, the High Court has both a civil and criminal jurisdiction. In civil matters, it hears cases to the value of £50,000 or above. In criminal matters it hears appeals against conviction or sentence. To assist this dual role, the High Court, part of the Supreme Court of England and Wales, is divided into three separate divisions:

▶ **Queens Bench Division** (QBD) – Considers claims in contract and tort. Hears criminal appeals, judicial review applications and proceedings. It has an Admiralty court and Commercial court to dispense with its business.

▶ **Chancery Division** (Ch) – Considers matters about property, trusts, probate and business matters. The Vice Chancellor presides over this division.

▶ **Family Division** (Fam Div) – Considers matrimonial and domestic causes, such as adoption, wardship and divorce. It is presided over by a President.

Building and civil engineering matters are dealt with by the high

court in 'Official Referees' matters. In the High Court, the first
rank of senior judges are called High Court judges. They are
appointed by the monarch and knighted on appointment. They
hear cases and are referred to as 'Mr/Mrs Justice [surname]'.
Appeals from the High Court lie to the higher courts.

The Appeal Court

To simplify matters, appeals in the higher courts are divided
between their respective divisions: the civil, or criminal.

1. In the Court of Appeal (Criminal Division), the Lord Chief
   Justice (LCJ), presently Lord Bingham, presides. He is
   accompanied by another two judges.

2. In the Court of Appeal (Civil Division) the Master of the Rolls
   (MR), currently Lord Woolf, presides. He sits with two other
   judges.

All appeals must be based on grounds of law. Appeals are heard by
three judges, all of whom are Lord Justices. Appeals lie (with
leave) to the House of Lords or to the European Court of Justice
(ECJ). The Court of Appeal sits in the Royal Courts of Justice in
The Strand in London.

The House of Lords

The highest court in the UK is the House of Lords. It hears
appeals from all the courts below, including the Court of Appeal,
the High Court and others, and including the Northern Irish and
Scottish courts.

All appeals are heard by at least three law lords, and normally
by five. Each law lord expresses his opinion of the case. Since 1833
the House of Lords has also had an extra-territorial jurisdiction.
As the Judicial Committee of the Privy Council it hears appeals
from courts in the former British colonies.

Furthermore, until recently, another court existed in the House
of Lords. This was a special court. It sat where the court itself, by
its own motion, deemed it necessary to decide whether a re-
hearing of a case should take place for exceptional reasons. This

arose in the extradition hearing of the former Chilean President, General Pinochet (see Bartle and Evans v. The Commissioner of Police for the Metropolis, ex parte Pinochet (1998) 25 November). The House of Lords decided that a re-hearing should take place and its previous decision set aside because one of the law lords had failed to sufficiently disclose an interest or membership of an organisation (Amnesty International) which was a joined party to the proceedings.

Civil courts reform and Lord Woolf

In 1995 Lord Woolf published his report, *Access to Justice*. This report investigated persons' access to civil justice, for example suing and other forms of civil litigation. Since 26th April 1999, the so-called 'Woolf Reforms' have come into force and 'civil justice' now requires:

(a) there should be a fast track procedure for all cases up to £10,000

(b) maximum legal costs for the fast track cases should be £2,500

(c) alternative dispute resolution should be enhanced, in order to encourage more parties to settle their civil disputes

Such reforms have been welcomed both by the legal profession and by various legal charities. These reforms arise at an interesting time politically, given that the present Labour government is intent on cutting public spending. In particular the government is committed to cutting the legal aid budget, especially the amounts claimed by highly paid QCs. Overall, the Woolf reforms aim to lower the cost of litigation and discourage litigation in the first place. They aim to encourage the parties to civil cases to settle their disputes, and to speed up the civil court process, in which cases can drag on expensively for years.

The prisons system

The current prison population in the UK numbers around 63,000 prisoners. This statistic bears witness to the fact that the likely outcome for many offenders in the British criminal justice system is **custody**. Prisons are governed by the 1952 Prison Act and are categorised according to their inmates (for example terrorists or low risk offenders) and location (local, high security, special units). Prison is for offenders over the age of 18. For younger offenders there are Young Offenders Institutions.

The Prison Rules

Under the 1952 Prison Act, the Home Secretary bears overall responsibility for prisons. Consequently, it is the Home Secretary's job to enforce the **Prison Rules**, which govern the conduct and disciplinary matters in prisons. The 1964 Prison Rules set out a list of privileges, rights and general terms of governance of prisoners whilst incarcerated in British prisons. Similarly, the management of young offenders in custody is governed by the Young Offenders Institution Rules of 1988. All of these Prison Rules were amended in 1998.

Prisons management and inspection

Apart from the Home Secretary, there exists a framework of prison monitoring, checks and inspection. These duties are undertaken by a number of bodies:

▶ *prison governors* – The governor is the legal custodian of the prison and the person who controls the day-to-day activities of the prison, its staff and inmates.

▶ *prison visitors* – These are independent lay persons who visit the prison and hear prisoner complaints. They take up complaints with the prison governor).

▶ *The Prisons Ombudsperson* – This office was set up in 1994. The prisoner has direct access to this official in order to resolve a grievance if all internal procedures for complaining have been exhausted.

▶ *The Prisons Inspectorate* – The Chief Inspector of Prisons has a duty to inspect all prisons and to report to the Home Secretary on the conditions which exist in British prisons.

Prisoner's rights are important, being covered by articles 2, 3 and 5 of the 1950 European Convention on Human Rights.

Reforms

The 1992 Woolf Report into Prisons brought about significant changes to the life of the prisoner in British prisons. Most notably, it improved the physical environment of the prisoner, in particular the sanitation and overcrowding. Since 1994, however, some prisons have been contracted out to private service providers, such as Group 4 and Securicor. Whilst these prisons continue under the Home Secretary's supervisory powers, different practices and regimes can now exist.

Parole

Parole is a prisoner's right to early release for 'good behaviour'. This right was radically reformed by 1991 Criminal Justice Act. A Parole Board meets to consider applications for parole by prisoners. Successful applicants are now released on 'licence'. This means that after about 26 weeks after their release a review is undertaken. If the former prisoner reoffends within those 26, he or she is returned to custody.

Tagging

Lastly, since 20 January 1998, a new system of tagging offenders has been introduced, as an alternative to custody. Tagging is a telephonic monitoring system, which relays information about the offender's location and conduct. It is expected that the introduction of tagging will not only lower the future prison population, but – when applied to existing prison inmates – could reduce the current prison population significantly.

Tutorial

Practice questions

The following questions will help you to revise and understand the national courts system:

1. What is meant by the term 'civil courts'?

2. What are the functions of the criminal courts?

3. List *three* civil and criminal courts. Briefly describe the typical day-to-day judicial business and powers of each.

4. List all the major British courts and outline their powers and jurisdiction.

5. What role do magistrates play in the English courts system?

6. If you are not sure how to answer any of these questions, then spend a few minutes reading this chapter again.

Seminar discussion

1. Why should it be necessary to have separate civil and criminal courts? Should this twin system of justice continue indefinitely, or should a way be found to unify it?

2. How far are the courts decision-takers, and how far are they policy-makers?

3. 'The House of Lords is not a court, it is a policy body.' Would you agree? Back up your arguments using examples of the law lords' judicial activities.

Further reading

Bailey & Gunn, *The Modern English Legal System* (3ed.), (1997), Sweet & Maxwell.

Williams, *Learning the Law* (11ed., 2nd impression), (1990), Stevens.

Slapper & Kelly, *Principles of the English Legal System* (3ed.), (1997), Cavendish.

Ingman, Learning Legal Skills (2ed.), (1997), Blackstones.

Stern, *Bricks of Shame*, (1989), Penguin.

Leech, *The Prisons Handbook*, (1997), Pluto Press.

5

European Institutions and Law

One minute summary – In 1973 the UK entered the European Economic Community (EEC). This organisation has since evolved into the European Union (EU), and UK law has now been superseded by European Community law. This means that British lawyers and law students must now be aware not just of domestic laws, but of EU laws as well. In this chapter you will learn how European law and the various EU institutions impact upon the English legal system. In addition, the supra-national nature of British law will be examined. In particular, the law-making roles of the European Courts of Justice and Human Rights will be analysed. This chapter will cover:

▶ the emergence of Community law
▶ the EU institutions today
▶ the supremacy of European law
▶ the European Convention and Court of Human Rights

The emergence of Community law

The pervasive influence of European Union law is becoming more apparent with each year that passes. Lord Denning once described it as 'an ever-flowing tide'. This tide has been flowing along under the original Treaty of Rome ever since 1957. Under this Treaty, now recast as the Treaty on European Union, laws are made which affect and bind the UK, following its admission to membership in 1973. European Community law is now supreme and prevails over United Kingdom law.

The European Union consists of 15 member states: Austria, Belgium, Denmark, France, Iceland, Ireland, Italy, Germany, Greece, Luxembourg, Netherlands, Portugal, Spain, Sweden and the United Kingdom. It is expected that Hungary and Poland will accede to the EU sometime in 2000.

This organisation of European states was first set up in 1957 under the Treaty of Rome. Known as the **European Economic Community** (EEC), its aim was to maintain peace, and to reconstruct and unite the nations of Europe after the devastation of the second world war (1939–45). The EEC sought to establish a 'common market' area for trade.

Following a growth in its membership, and its success as a trading area between the 1950s and 1970s, it was replaced in the 1980s by the **European Community** (EC). This new entity sought to foster not just economic but ever-closer political union among its twelve member states.

Eventually, at the Maastricht Summit in 1992, the activities of the EC were widened further to include cultural, industrial, employment, public health, consumer protection and environmental co-operation. The EC now became the **European Union**, reflecting its new far-reaching social agenda, as well as its original post-war economic goals and political aims. In 1998, after the Amsterdam Summit, the revised Treaty on European Union, extended the economic, social and political goals to ease the (closer) union of the European Peoples.

The EU institutions today

Under the foundation Treaty of the Union – the Treaty of Rome (1957) – four principal institutions were listed: the Commission, the Council, the Parliament, and the Court of Justice.

The European Commission

Based in Brussels, the Commission is the permanent body of officials of the EU. It is not unlike the UK civil service. It consists of twenty commissioners, each a representative of a member state. The five major EU member states each have two commissioners, rather than just one. The UK commissioners are currently Christopher Patten and Neil Kinnock. Each commissioner has charge of an area of policy and a directorate-general, the department of officials responsible for it. Directorate-generals range from external affairs, economic affairs, internal market, social affairs, agriculture, transport, fisheries to regional policy, energy, science, budgets and development.

The role of the Commission is to initiate and draft legislation and to enforce it, where they hold the powers to do so.

The European Council

According to the Treaty, the Council shall consist of 'a representative of each member state' responsible for the policy area being discussed. Hence, the composition of this institution varies according to which issue is being discussed. The ministers responsible from each member state attend the discussion to put their country's view. For example, when financial or economic matters are being discussed, the UK would send the chancellor of the exchequer. On farming issues it would send the agriculture minister.

Member states also take it in turns to chair the Council meetings for six months at a time. This chairship is termed the 'Presidency' of the Council. This institution is assisted by a permanent secretariat of civil servants and advisers, and by a committee of permanent representatives. The latter, known as COREPER, consists of each member state's ambassador to the EU, who represents their country in the EU on a daily basis.

The European Parliament

The European Parliament (EP) is the democratically elected organ of the EU. This institution is composed of elected members of the European Parliament (MEPs). There are 624 in all, directly elected since 1979 from fifteen member states. MEPs sit in broad political groupings, much as in the UK parliament (but without regard to nationality). The main EU political groupings in the EP are the:

Socialist group, including UK Labour party
Christian Democrats, including the UK Conservative party
Liberal Democratic and Reformist group, including the UK Liberal Democrats
Greens
Rainbow Alliance group
Fascists
Radical Left group
other small groups

The EP has a legislative role, carried out with its various committees. While it does not initiate legislation, it can approve or reject legislative proposals submitted by the EU Commission and Council. It also debates important issues in its plenary sessions. These take place one week per month, and are held in either Strasbourg or Brussels.

The Court of Justice

Based in Luxembourg, the European Court of Justice (ECJ) is the legal institution of the European Union. It consists of the Court of First Instance, which hears competition cases and internal staff matters, and the Court of Justice itself. Its chief role is to interpret and uphold the Treaty.

The court's judicial function includes making sure that all member states have properly implemented European law. In terms of enforcement, the ECJ is assisted by the Commission, which initiates proceedings against recalcitrant member states.

There are fifteen judges in all. The ECJ delivers a single collegiate judgement, upon which the ECJ as a whole has agreed. The ECJ is aided by an independent rapporteur, an Advocate-General who advises the ECJ and gives his opinion. The court can accept that opinion, or not. Since 1957, the ECJ has developed much case law, but is *not* bound by this in future cases. This unusual lack of precedents – unusual in English terms – makes the court both unpredictable and robust in its rulings.

Other European institutions

Other institutions in the European Union include the:

▶ *Court of Auditors* – the body responsible for the EU's large budgets and accounting.

▶ *European Council* – the forum in which the heads of government, namely prime ministers or presidents of the member states, meet to discuss matters.

▶ *Economic and Social Committee* – an advisory body to both the EU Commission and Council. It represents business and the unions, and issues opinions and reports on various proposed pieces of legislation.

▶ *Committee of the Regions* – the newest of the institutions. It represents regional and local bodies such as councils, and again is an advisory body which issues reports on various issues and proposed legislation.

Clearly, the European Union is a supra-national body. It has a superstructure of multifaceted institutions tasked with policy-making and law-making within all its territories.

The supremacy of European law

The supremacy of European law has been the subject of the most controversial legal debate this century. This question of its legal supremacy can be viewed from both a European and an English perspective.

The European point of view

The European Court of Justice (ECJ) has consistently claimed that European law prevails and is supreme over national law. This claim was first established in 1963 in a case called *Van Gend en Loos*. Since *Van Gend en Loos* the ECJ has ruled that, by accepting EU membership, *all* member states have transferred from their domestic legal systems the rights and obligations under the Treaty to the EU. Since 1963 the ECJ has therefore argued that, where any domestic law is incompatible with a European law, the European law prevails.

In practice this means that EU law only prevails where there are inconsistencies within the national, domestic legal regime of a member state. Where no inconsistency arise, domestic law continues to prevail.

The English point of view

In contrast to the EU view, the British standpoint was historically to support a separate system of law, in which domestic law prevails and cannot be challenged. This view was expressed in 1971 by Lord Denning in *Blackburn v. Attorney General*. In this case Denning stated that: 'these [British] courts should take no notice of treaties as such.' This statement was made before the UK entered the EU.

However, for some years after its admission to the EEC (as it was in 1973), the English courts followed Denning's guidance.

This conflict between European and domestic law continued intermittently for some twenty years. The statute which enabled Britain's entry into the EU – the European Communities Act (1972) – did not state which law, European or English, was to prevail. In the absence of such a supremacy clause, the courts had to interpret and determine which law prevailed. In time, this led to such cases being referred to the ECJ to provide guidance. This practice in itself led to a resolution of the debate.

Resolving the supremacy dispute

Such disparate views have inevitably given rise to much case law on the relationship between English and European law:

(a) One example can be found in the many sex discrimination cases from 1975 onwards.

(b) Another example is the now renowned case of Factortame (see *R v. Secretary of State for Transport, ex parte Factortame Ltd [1998] (No. 5) The Times, 28 April 1998.* This case involved Spanish trawlermen fishing in British waters. It conclusively affirms the supremacy of European law over domestic English law.

The supremacy of European law creates a unique and wide-ranging opportunity for fourteen other EU states to influence various aspects of English life through law.

The European Convention and Court of Human Rights

Outside the remit of Community or EU law there lies an international dimension of human rights. This arises under the UN's Universal Declaration of Human Rights, and at a European level under the 1950 European Convention on Human Rights (ECHR). Drafted in 1949, the ECHR asserts these fundamental human rights, among others:

(a) the right to life
(b) freedom from inhuman and degrading treatment
(c) the right to liberty and security of person
(d) the right to a fair and public hearing
(e) the right to privacy
(f) freedom of expression
(g) the right to protest
(h) the right to marry and have a family

This convention, of which the UK is a signatory, has had a huge impact on British law. In particular, the ECHR has had a big impact on prisoners' rights and police powers in the UK. Until recently, the ECHR had not been incorporated into English law, despite many previous attempts by leading human rights campaigners.

However, in November 1998 the UK government fully incorporated the ECHR into English law as part of its Human Rights Act 1998. This ends the debate about the legal status of the ECHR. It affirms the courts' long held view that when English law is ambiguous the ECHR ought to be applied anyway (see *Derbyshire County Council v. The Times Newspapers*, [1993] The Times, 19 February). The 1998 Human Rights Act fully comes into force in October 2000.

The ECHR deals with some very important human rights. As a law student you must be aware that UK and other citizens, whose home countries are signatories to the ECHR, may have recourse to the law under the ECHR. The Commission of Human Rights – the filtering body which decides whether cases will be heard or not – and the European Court of Human Rights, in Strasbourg, seek to enforce these human rights.

Tutorial

Practice questions
The following questions will help to revise and learn about European law and institutions:

1. Which are the major EU law-making institutions?

2. How far has European law created a new legal order within the English legal system?

3. List the four principal institutions of the EU. Define the main functions of each.

4. What is the legislative role of the European Parliament?

5. Briefly summarise human rights law. How does it complement existing British domestic liberties?

If you are not sure how to answer any of these questions, then spend a few minutes reading this chapter again.

Seminar discussion

1. How great has been the impact of the 1950 European Convention on Human Rights on English law?

2. 'If European law is supreme, we should abolish English law altogether.' Use examples to back up your arguments for or against.

3. Does it matter how far the British public supports the laws and institutions of the European Union?

Further reading

Craig & De Burca, *EC Law: Text, Cases & Materials* (2ed.), (1998), Oxford.
Weatheril & Beamount, *EC Law*, (1996), Penguin.
Clements, *European Human Rights*, (1997), Sweet & Maxwell.
Harris, O'Boyle & Warbrick, *Law of the European Convention on Human Rights*, (1997), Butterworths.

6

The British Legal Profession

One minute summary – Most members of the British judiciary are appointed from the legal profession. They are therefore legally qualified and are often referred to as the 'professional' judiciary. In this chapter you will learn which lawyers exist in the English legal system, what services they offer, what training they have, and who governs them. The chapter will cover:

► solicitors
► barristers
► legal education
► criticisms of the UK legal profession
► the professional bodies
► reform – fusion of the profession?

Unlike elsewhere in Europe and the United States of America, within the UK its legal profession, in other words its lawyers or legal services, are divided into two distinct branches: Solicitors and Barristers.

Solicitors

There are more than 70,000 solicitors in the UK today. Established and regulated since 1605, solicitors make up the largest of the two branches within the UK legal profession. Solicitors are governed by the Law Society, under the Solicitors Acts of 1843 and 1974. As general practitioners of law, solicitors can advise the public directly on a range of both criminal and civil matters. In reality, most solicitors' firms now specialise. Still true to their historical roots, solicitors administer legal aid and can represent clients before the courts up to the Crown Court, subject to obtaining the necessary certification.

A varied profession

There are many kinds of solicitors in practice. They include partners of city or provincial firms, specialist, or employed solicitors. Unlike barristers, solicitors are organised in 'firms' working in offices, even if they may be sole practitioners. Such a description is an accident of history, since it is supposed to depict the major point of distinction between the two branches of the profession: that is, solicitors can advertise their services whilst barristers cannot. Furthermore, solicitors 'instruct' barristers. That is, the public cannot directly go to a barrister for services, whereas they can to a solicitor.

The business with which solicitors can deal is also very different, depending upon the type of firm you go to. For instance, some law firms specialise in business and commercial law only. Others may specialise in medical negligence, European, property (conveyancing work), family, criminal or personal injuries. Other law firms cover all of these and more, or solely provide services in a few areas of litigation only. Since the introduction of legal aid franchising, solicitors' firms have a tendency to specialise more according to which franchise they hold.

Barristers

Barristers-at-Law are governed by the Bar Council and the four Inns of Court (Gray's Inn, Inner Temple, Lincoln's Inn and Middle Temple). More generally just called 'barristers' today, they have existed since medieval times. Barristers are the advocates of the UK legal profession, and hold rights of audience before all the courts within the UK. Until 1990 and the enactment of the Courts and Legal Services Act, barristers held the monopoly of appearing in the higher courts.

Today some 14,000 barristers practise in the UK. There is an increasing tendency for barristers to specialise, but some still have 'common law practices': this means that they provide services which cover many different areas of litigation, such as crime, family, negligence and contractual matters.

Chambers

Barristers practise from chambers (not offices). A set of chambers is a collective of self-employed barristers who share the services of a clerk. A clerk to chambers seeks work for 'his' barristers from local solicitors. The clerk is usually paid according to the amount of work he obtains for the barrister, receiving a set fee or/and percentage of the fees received from that work.

Circuits

Barristers practise on circuits, which are geographically defined areas. There are six main circuits in England and Wales: the Midland and Oxford, Northern, North Eastern, Wales and Chester, Western, and South Eastern circuits.

Rules of professional conduct

As to conduct, barristers must be independent in their practice. They must not engage in 'dishonest or other acts of misconduct which will discredit the profession'. Similarly, these rules apply to solicitor's conduct. Most significantly, barristers are not allowed to refuse to represent someone. This rule, the so-called 'cab-rank rule' has been in existence for centuries. Its purpose is to ensure the fundamental right to representation of the accused in criminal trials.

Barristers and their clients

The main restriction on barristers is that they are not permitted to have direct professional access to the client. However, special exemptions exist for barristers who work in law centres. In addition, barristers may promote their services, but not by direct advertising. Furthermore, a practising barrister may not enter into a partnership with another practising barrister. The English Bar remains a profession of individual practitioners.

Queen's Counsel

A distinctive feature of the English Bar is the ranking of its members into junior counsel and Queen's Counsel (QC). The letters patent QC identify the more senior and able members of the profession. The appointment of QC is made by the monarch. The elevation to QC, or 'silk' as it is colloquially known, means that senior practitioners can focus their practice on the more important, complex, high profile and remunerative cases. As well as meaning recognition by your peers, and less paperwork, it also opens up further opportunities, such as elevation to the more senior judiciary (to be discussed in the next chapter).

Legal education

As to legal education, members of both branches of the UK legal profession must hold an academic qualification in law. They must also have passed professional examinations, regulated by their respective professional bodies, and undertake continuing post-qualification professional education. See the summary provided by figure 6 on page 46.

Solicitors
(a) Prospective solicitors usually hold a law degree, or a degree and a diploma in law. The diploma is usually the Common Professional Examination (CPE) for non-law graduates.

(b) They must also have completed their Law Practice Course (LPC), a professional examination regulated by the Law Society, and once known as the Law Society Finals examination.

(c) They must also have been enrolled on the Solicitor's Roll.

Law Practice Courses
The Law Practice Courses are now franchised to many universities across the UK. Since 1993 the LPC is no longer the monopoly of the Law Society's Colleges of Law at Guildford, Chester, Store Street in London (the latter was formerly at two sites in London: Chancery Lane and Lancaster Gate), and York. LPCs are intended to ensure that the prospective solicitor can professionally practise in both civil and criminal litigation, is a competent advocate and is able to give advise, negotiate and draft documents, as well as to understand professional conduct and ethical issues.

Barristers' training
Similarly, to become a barrister the student must be a law

graduate or equivalent, be a member of one of the four Inns of Court, and have completed the Bar's Vocational course. Again this course is a practice-focused one covering advocacy, drafting, negotiating, procedure and evidence.

In the past, a Bar student had to consume between 18 and 26 dinners at their Inn before they could be called to the Bar. Students were also required to attend the Inns of Court School of Law, located in London, in order to complete their vocational course.

Like the LPC, decentralisation has taken place since 1997. Today, several universities across the UK offer this course outside London. At present they include the University of Northumbria at Newcastle, the University of the West of England, the Oxford Centre for Legal Studies, and Manchester Metropolitan University.

Criticisms of the UK legal profession

As a student of law you need to be aware that many criticisms have been levelled at the UK legal profession and judiciary over the years. Many critics say that the profession does not properly reflect modern society. These criticisms have raised issues of social background, gender and race inequality.

Various reports have been published on the profession, and on the judiciary in particular. They tend to show the following points:

1. Very few women are members of the legal profession. Only one female judge sits in the Court of Appeal, and no women sit in a higher court.

2. The English legal profession generally reflects a membership drawn from a narrow (middle or upper class) social background.

3. Few persons of black and ethnic minority origin are judges or members of the legal profession.

Both the Bar Council and the Law Society – as well as the Equal Opportunities Commission and the Commission for Racial Equality – are concerned about this. Moreover, the Judicial

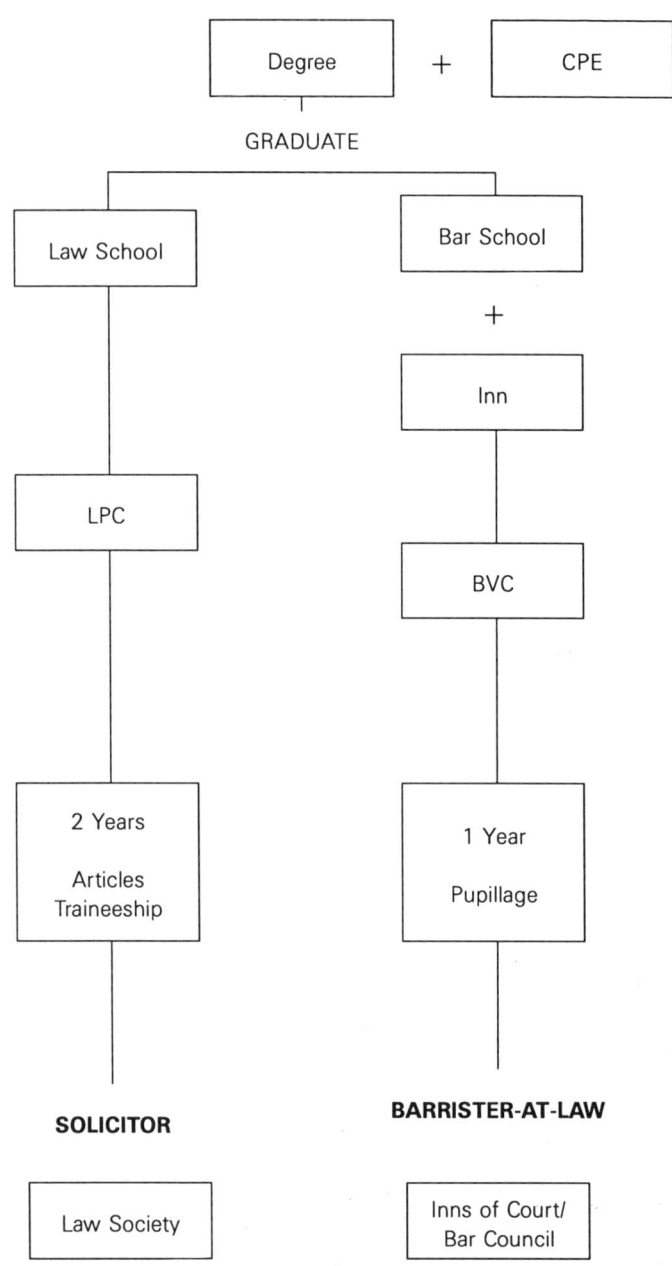

Fig. 6. Becoming a lawyer:
a summary of English legal education.

Studies Board (which trains judges) has sought in more recent years to carry out equal opportunities awareness and training. Many of the groups outlined still feel under-represented today, but at least the issues are being raised and give rise to some optimism for the future.

The professional bodies

Given the UK profession's membership is large, both historically and even more today, the English legal profession was in need of organisation and regulation. Consequently, professional bodies evolved from the development and modernisation of both the Bar and solicitors' profession. Today, barristers and solicitors are governed by their respective bodies, the Bar Council and the Law Society.

The Law Society

Solicitors have been regulated ever since 1605. In 1833 the old Society of Attorneys, Solicitors and Proctors changed its name to the Law Society. The Solicitors Act of 1843 regulated solicitors' conduct, and required a register of its members to be kept. A barrister – the Master of the Rolls, a senior judge – has the official responsibility for admitting persons to become solicitors. The Law Society, however, remains responsible for issuing so-called 'practising certificates'. Under ss.1, 9–18 of the Solicitors Act 1974 a person must hold one of these in order to practise law as a solicitor.

The Law Society's organisation is hierarchical. It has a President, elected annually by its membership. The President presides over the Council of the Law Society. The powers of the Law Society are now derived from the Solicitors Act 1974. In particular, the Law Society is responsible for the conduct of its members. In particular, its Solicitors Disciplinary Tribunal and Solicitors' Complaints Bureau seek to ensure that incompetent solicitors are removed from the Solicitors' Roll and are denied a practising certificate in the future. The Solicitors' Code of Conduct and Solicitor's Rule provide a common code of conduct and practice for these purposes.

The Bar Council

The collective term for barristers is 'the English Bar'. The Bar has remained largely unregulated by government over the centuries. The Bar was mainly governed by the four separate Inns of Court and their benchers. Benchers were their most senior practising barristers and/or judges. The benchers were responsible for establishing good practice. Furthermore, the judges were expected, through the law courts, to exercise control of practice.

The independence of the Inns of Court was reduced in the 1980s. Barristers are now governed by the General Council of the Bar of England and Wales. This body consists of 107 members, including officers of the Council, such as its chairperson (elected annually by its rank and file), leaders of the circuits, and elected representatives. The Bar Council's major roles are to:

(a) register those called to the Bar

(b) discipline its members for misconduct

(c) represent the interests of its members in the wider public domain

The dual role of (b) and (c) has often attracted criticism. The Bar Council now governs the education of barristers in cooperation with the Council of the Inns of Court and the Council of Legal Education.

Better future regulation?

Since the enactment of the Courts and Legal Services Act 1990, the Law Society and Bar Council have not entirely been responsible for their self-regulation. Under the 1990 Act, other bodies and officials have a role to play. These include the Lord Chancellor's Advisory Committee on Legal Education and Conduct (ACLEC), and the Director of Fair Trading. These ensure that the appropriate entry qualifications and education, standards of service and fair competition exists within the legal profession.

From 1990 onwards, there has been a Legal Services Ombudsperson. See Chapter 9 for further detailed information on 'ombudspersons'. Users of legal services users can contact this public official to complain about the level of services which they have received (see s. 20 of the Courts and Legal Services Act).

Reform – fusion of the profession?

Rule 7(6) of the Solicitor's Practice Rules 1990, says that a solicitor may employ, but may not form a partnership with, a member of another profession. The exception to this rule is multi-national legal practitioners. Subject to s. 66 of the Courts and Legal Services Act 1990, UK solicitors can now engage in practices with registered solicitors from countries outside the UK. There are at present some 60 multinational practices. Many of these cover the various countries of the EU. Such a rule and practice ensures that an English tradition is preserved in the delivery of legal services.

Today we have a divided legal profession, made up of two branches, barristers and solicitors, each offering different services. Whilst each branch of the profession undertakes advisory work, litigation and drafting, the functions of each are established and distinct. Even the 1969 Royal Commission heard arguments that a joined – so called fused – profession be established. This it rejected in view of the advantages of current practice, in particular the independent nature of both professionals.

Later scrutiny under the 1988 Marre Committee concurred with the conclusions of the earlier Royal Commission and tended to recommend against fusion of the two halves.

The 1990 Courts and Legal Services Act

However, some changes came about as a result of the 1990 Courts and Legal Services Act. Parts II and IV of this Act sought to bring closer together the provision of legal services by two distinct professions. Most notably, the Act established a legal services ombudsman which covered both branches of the profession. It gave a statutory basis to the Lord Chancellor's advisory committee on legal education and conduct, which now covered the training and regulation of both professions; and it extended the rights of audience of suitably qualified persons, including solicitors.

Since both professional bodies' rules and practices have been subjected to review, one wonders as we enter the new millennium whether a fused profession will be attained sometime in the future.

Tutorial

Practice questions
The following questions will help you to revise and learn about the English legal profession:

1. What regulatory bodies exist to govern the English legal profession? What professional rules of conduct do they apply?

2. How are lawyers trained in the UK?

3. Summarise what distinguishes solicitors and barristers in their

   (a) professional role
   (b) method of working

4. 'English lawyers are white, public school educated men'. Consider this view in light of the criticisms of the English legal profession. Explain what is being done to rectify these criticisms.

If you are not sure how to answer any of these questions, then spend a few minutes reading this chapter again.

Seminar discussion
1. 'The English legal profession is really one, divided'. Do you agree?

2. What inequalities exist within the English legal profession and what action about them should be taken?

Further reading
Bailey & Gunn, *The Modern English Legal System* (3ed.), (1997), Sweet & Maxwell.
Abel & Lewis (eds.), *Lawyers in Society* (2ed.), (1996), Sweet & Maxwell.
Royal Commission on Legal Services (1969), HMSO.
Pannick, *Advocates* (1996), OUP.
Griffiths, *The Politics of the Judiciary* (1996), Penguin.

7

The British Judiciary and Law Officers

One minute summary – Over the centuries, events in English legal history have led to the creation of a variety of types of legal office holders. The most significant of these are the judges. In this chapter we will examine the various types of judges, their judicial roles, and how both lay and professional people play a part within the English judiciary. In this chapter you will learn about magistrates and judges, the senior judiciary including the Lord Chancellor, Lord Chief Justice, Master of the Rolls, the hierarchy of the judges, and the role of law officers in the English legal system. The chapter will cover:

▶ the judiciary
▶ the senior judges
▶ the magistracy
▶ the judicial hierarchy
▶ the law officers
▶ judicial office holders and the role of the judiciary

The judiciary

The word 'judiciary' is the collective term for the persons appointed to adjudicate in courts or tribunals upon disputes. A remarkable feature of the British judiciary is that so much of it – some 50,000 members of it – is lay. This feature is derived from Magna Carta 1215, when it was affirmed that trial by peers should be an essential part of the legal system. We will now consider who makes up the judiciary and what powers they have.

The lay judiciary

The laity plays a significant, but limited, role in the British judiciary. Lay members serve in two main ways, as:

▶ **magistrates** – Lay magistrates deal with 98 per cent of criminal matters and other civil disputes, as discussed in previous chapters. They receive no payment other than travel expenses.

▶ **members of tribunals** – Tribunal members are appointed regionally and sit in a variety of local tribunals. Again, they receive no payment except travel expenses.

As lay people, both magistrates and members of tribunals receive training and monitoring. In the magistrates' courts they are assisted by legally qualified clerks, and in the tribunals by chairwomen/men. The work of tribunals will be discussed in the next chapter.

The professional judiciary

Before the enactment of the 1990 Courts and Legal Services Act, appointment as a judge was confined to barristers. Nowadays, additional rules govern appointments, such as age, experience, qualifications and quotas. These will be discussed below. However, appointment to the senior judiciary requires the appointee/ judicial office-holder to be a legally qualified practitioner, in other words either a solicitor or barrister. Consequently, in the higher courts, above magistrates level, there is a professional judiciary made up of experienced law practitioners.

The senior judges

Members of the 'senior judiciary' consist of anyone who holds office of High Court judge or above. Within this grouping are the most senior of judges who sit in the higher courts discussed earlier.

The Lord Chancellor

The Lord Chancellor is the highest judicial office holder in the English legal system. He – there has yet to be a woman – is also a cabinet minister and Speaker in the House of Lords. The Lord Chancellor has overall responsibility within the English legal system for

(a) the administration of the courts
(b) the supervision of legal aid
(c) judicial appointments

In addition to his historical powers, the Lord Chancellor is also responsible under the 1990 Courts and Legal Services Act for legal education and conduct, the ombudsmen system, and for law reform. In these various roles, he is helped by staff from the Lord Chancellor's Department (LCD). Since the 1950s this has grown in size into a large organisation employing over 12,000 staff. Since 1992 the Lord Chancellor has also had a parliamentary secretary in the House of Commons. This is an MP of junior minister rank who answers questions on his behalf.

The current Lord Chancellor is Lord Irvine of Lairg QC, and his parliamentary secretary is Keith Vaz MP. Apart from this complex web of both political, ceremonial and judicial duties, the Lord Chancellor occasionally sits as a judge, and is in fact a law lord in the judicial committee of the House of Lords.

The Lord Chief Justice

The role of Lord Chief Justice of England (LCJ) is to be the head of and to administer the criminal courts in the UK. The LCJ's day-to-day function is to preside over the

(a) Criminal Appeals Division of the Court of Appeal, and
(b) Queen's Bench Division of the High Court

The office of LCJ was created under the Judicature Acts of 1873-75. The appointment is made by the Queen, having consulted the Prime Minister. By convention the Prime Minister in turn seeks the advice of the Lord Chancellor. The appointment is usually made from the ranks of the High Court bench or above. An existing Court of Appeal judge is normally chosen. The LCJ issues directions on criminal justice practice, and issues guidance on sentencing. The present LCJ is Lord Thomas Bingham of Cornhill.

The Master of the Rolls

The Master of the Rolls (MR) is an historical office and title, dating back to the thirteenth century. Its name derives from the function of keeping the register ('roll') of practising solicitors (see chapter 6). Today, this judicial office-holder is head of, and administers, the civil courts. He presides over the civil division of the Court of Appeal. The MR is also responsible for civil law reform. The current MR is Lord Woolf.

Law lords

The law lords, or Lords of Appeal in Ordinary as they are more formally titled, are appointed from practitioners of fifteen or more years' standing. They must have held high judicial office (High Court judge or above) for two years or more. By convention, two of the law lords are Scottish lawyers. The maximum number of law lords is twelve at any one time. These judges are the most senior in the British legal system, including both the Scottish and Northern Irish jurisdictions. They sit in the judicial committee of the House of Lords. The law lords normally sit in courts of five, or occasionally seven, judges.

Lord Justices of Appeal

The maximum number of Lord Justices of Appeal, or appellate court judges as they are more widely known, is thirty-five. Appointments to the Court of Appeal are usually made from the ranks of existing High Court judges. A candidate is normally a practitioner of over ten years' standing and a sitting High Court judge. These judges sit in the Court of Appeal, comprised ordinarily of three appellate judges.

High Court judges

Appointments to the High Court bench are normally made from the ranks of Queen's Counsel, that is senior barristers or 'silks' with over twenty years' legal practice. However, following reforms under the 1990 Courts and Legal Services Act, High Court judges can be appointed from persons who have held the right of audience before the High Court for over ten years, or who have been a circuit judge for two or more years. The maximum number of High Court judges is ninety-eight. They were historically called 'puisne' judges, a Latin term indicating that they travelled from place to place to administer justice.

Appointees to the High Court are often assigned to its various divisions:

(a) Chancery Division
(b) Queen's Bench Division
(c) Family Division

Appointment to these divisions often reflects the former law practitioner's area of expertise. Additional offices exist within the High Court, such as President of the Family Division, or Vice-Chancellor, or President of the Supreme Court. These latter posts are *ex officio* members of the Court of Appeal.

Circuit judges

The circuit bench was created under the Courts Act 1971. This allowed crown court and county court judges to be appointed from among solicitors or barristers of more than ten years' practice. Those who had served as a recorder for three years or more also became eligible. For further details of recorders, see 7.2.8, below.

Subject to s.71 of the Courts and Legal Services Act 1990, a practitioner must have 10 or more years' experience of crown court or county court work to qualify for appointment to the circuit bench. Once appointed, the new judge is assigned to a specific crown or county court where he or she will sit until retirement, promotion, or removal.

Recorders, district judges and stipendiary magistrates

Recorders

Recorders are part-time crown court judges. They are appointed to a specific court, for a fixed duration and number of days they must sit. These appointments are normally made for three years at a time. Recorders usually have ten or more years' practice.

District judges

District judges are part-time judges in the county court and are appointed from practitioners of seven or more years standing. Another county court part-time appointment is that of deputy district judge.

Stipendiary magistrates

There are more than 100 stipendiary magistrates in the UK. These appointees are the full or part-time legally qualified justices of the peace. They were established in 1792, largely to replace notoriously corrupt magistrates sitting in certain parts of the British Isles. Given that background, legal commentators of that day, such as Blackstone and Coke, prophesied the end of the lay magistracy. As noted above, and to be discussed below, this is far from the case. The stipendiary bench sits very comfortably alongside the lay bench in today's modern magistrates' court. This is helped by the fact that they share the same duties.

Stipendiary magistrates are either appointed to London, the so-called metropolis (hence their title 'metropolitan stipendiary magistrate') or to the provinces, major towns such as Manchester, Newcastle, Birmingham, Liverpool and Bristol. Unlike lay magistrates they are appointed directly by the Lord Chancellor and not by local advisory committees. Stipendiary magistrates are appointed from legal practitioners, solicitors or barristers, of some seven or more year's practice experience. Because a stipendiary has practice experience, the role of the justices' clerk is simply to administer and not to advise the bench. Moreover, as the title 'stipendiary' suggests, they receive payment for their services, unlike lay magistrates. Currently, stipendiary magistrates receive a salary of about £67,000.

The magistracy

The magistracy was established long ago in 1361 under the Justices of the Peace Act. The magistrates are unpaid and receive the letters patent 'JP' after their name ('justice of the peace'). They can sit in magistrates' courts or with a judge in the crown court. They are appointed by the crown under the supervision of the Lord Chancellor or the Chancellor of the Duchy of Lancaster, for appointments in Lancashire, Greater Manchester and Merseyside, and by local advisory committees (105 of these committees exist in the UK). The only qualifications are that JPs must:

(a) reside within 15 miles of the court where they are appointed
(b) be of good standing in their local communities
(c) not be a bankrupt

The present Lord Chancellor, Lord Irvine, has announced that he wishes the magistracy to better reflect the communities they serve (See Lord Chancellor's press statement, Magistrates' Association Annual Conference, *Salford*, 17 November 1998). The only *ex officio* magistrates in the UK are the Lord Mayor and Aldermen of the City of London.

By historical enactment, the primary duty of a JP is to keep the peace. Hence, the title 'justice of the peace'. This duty explains why the advent of magistrates replaced the peace keepers (*custodes pacis*).

The work of the magistrates

The business of a magistrates' court, as discussed in previous chapters, is varied indeed. While primarily involved with adjudicating on petty criminal offences, magistrates also have powers in family matters and licensing. More significantly, they hold wide-ranging sentencing powers, including *inter alia*:

(a) absolute discharge
(b) imposing fines
(c) binding over
(d) community sentences
(e) placing on probation
(f) custodial sentences

On a day-to-day basis, JPs determine bail applications and the venue for criminal prosecutions. The Courts Act 1971 also provides that JPs can sit with crown court judges when hearing an appeal from the magistrates' court or conducting a trial where the person was committed for sentence from the magistrates court to the crown court. However, the Lord Chancellor, Lord Irvine, has recently announced his intention to remove the right of JPs to sit when sentencing is taking place. In any event, JPs must have completed two years of their basic training before being allowed to sit in the crown court with a judge.

Justices' clerks

Magistrates are assisted at all times by justices' clerks. These clerks are legally trained or qualified courtroom advisers and administrators. Justices' clerks are both responsible for the administration of the court business, that is its procedures, and act as legal adviser to the bench. Whilst the clerks will advise JPs, it is the magistrates themselves who make the determination. All magistrates are assisted by national sentencing guidelines issued by the Court of Appeal and the Magistrates' Association. The justices' clerk will therefore only advise on points of law, sentence, admissibility of evidence, and procedural issues. The magistrates will themselves decide upon the facts of a case, and its outcome.

Training of magistrates

Since 1953, all newly appointed magistrates have been required to attend training. This has included a triennium of activities and sessions of basic training. Having completed this in the first few years of appointment, refresher training has also been required since 1980. Since 1996, in order to become a chairwoman/man of the bench, further chairmanship training has to be undergone.

In 1998, these arrangements for training were replaced by the Judicial Studies Board which runs a competences-based training programme and mentorship by senior, experienced magistrates.

Retirement and disqualification

A JP can be removed from office on the grounds of infirmity, criminal conviction, misconduct or age. Seventy is the maximum upper age limit for retirement. Like all judges, magistrates are subject to the common law rules relating to disqualification. For example a JP holding a bias, or an interest in a particular case, is disqualified from determining that case.

The judicial hierarchy

All judicial appointments, except those of magistrates, are administered by the Judicial Appointments Committee of the Lord Chancellor's Department. The eligibility requirements for appointment, and the established quotas, are only revocable by an order of Parliament. This rigid judicial hierarchy, established over many years, is reinforced by the way in which each office confers on the holder its own particular title, prestige and power.

Hierarchical forms of address

(a) At the lowest level is the magistrate, whose office entitles the holder to place the letters 'JP' after his or her name.

(b) Circuit judges and recorders have the title 'His/Her Honour Judge...' or 'Mr/Mrs Recorder...' prefixing their surname.

(c) On appointment to the High Court the judge is knighted (if male) or made a Dame of the British Empire. The judge is referred to as 'Mr Justice [surname]' or Mrs Justice [surname]' respectively.

(d) Appeal court judges are referred to as 'Lord Justice [surname]'.

(e) Law lords are made life peers.

The modes of courtroom address form another distinctive feature of the English legal system. Again, this encourages a strong sense of hierarchy. For instance, for all High Court judges and above are addressed as 'My Lord', or as television programmes lead us to believe, 'M'Lud'. Circuit judges are referred to as 'Your Honour'. All judicial office-holders below the circuit bench are addressed as 'Sir or Madam (Ma'am)'. Magistrates are often referred to as 'Your Worships', a historical term dating back to medieval times.

According to Griffiths, the system of English judicial appointments tends to make the hierarchy a rigid and narrow one in terms of social class, education, ethnicity and gender. See Chapter 6 for more detailed on the criticisms of the English legal profession and judiciary. The whole system of accolades, titles and modes of address ensure that each part of the hierarchy retains great authority in the English legal system, irrespective of the power of a higher judge to set aside, quash or override the decision of a judge in the lower court.

The law officers

Another unique feature of the English legal system is its tradition of law officers. Law officers are defined as 'post-holders made by the crown for the performance of a specific duty'. Within the English legal system there are several principal law officers. They are discussed below:

The Attorney-General
The Attorney-General (AG) is the most senior law officer in the UK. The AG is a cabinet minister and usually an MP rather than a member of the House of Lords. He represents the government or 'the crown' as it is officially termed in proceedings before the European Court of Human Rights in Strasbourg, and the International Court in the Hague, or more commonly in the High Court or above.

The AG can himself institute proceedings, or consent to other cases proceeding in the public interest. He can also prevent trials from taking place at all. The AG is responsible for the Director of Public Prosecutions (DPP), the Crown Prosecution Service (CPS), and the Serious Fraud Office (SFO). In his work, the AG is assisted by a deputy, the Solicitor-General (SG), who is also usually an MP or peer, and by a legal secretariat.

The Director of Public Prosecutions
The office of the Director of Public Prosecutions (DPP) has existed since 1879. The duties of the DPP are statutorily defined in the Prosecution of Offences Act 1985. The DPP must be a lawyer of 10 years' experience. The DPP is responsible for the day-to-day conduct of the Crown Prosecution Service (CPS) and the Serious Fraud Office (SFO), established in 1985 and 1987 respectively. The DPP may represent the crown in appeals in the Court of Appeal or above.

The Official Solicitor
Like the DPP, the Official Solicitor (OS) must also be a lawyer of 10 years' standing. The OS is appointed under s.71 of the Courts and Legal Services Act 1990. He is responsible for:

(a) the application of *habeas corpus* and bail matters
(b) representing wards of court in wardship proceedings
(c) conducting litigation for children and mental patients
(d) administering the intestate estates of deceased persons
(e) assisting the court as *amicus curiae*

Home Secretary

The Home Secretary is best known as the cabinet minister responsible for law and order. However, in law officer terms, this Secretary of State is also responsible for prisons and the reform of criminal law under the remit of the Criminal Law Revision Committee. The Home Secretary also recommends the exercise or otherwise of the royal pardon, in order to quash a conviction or part of one.

Judicial office-holders and the role of the judiciary

Appointments

Appointments to the judicial offices and to the various law officers detailed above are nominally made by the Queen, having consulted the Prime Minister and/or Lord Chancellor. All of these appointments are subject to public criteria, and made on merit. Judicial appointments in particular require good character, and qualities such as common sense and a good track record, either as a legal practitioner or in the candidate's own employment or community. With retirement at age 70 for JPs and 76 for senior judges, the tenure of office of the judiciary clearly depends upon their good health, age and good conduct.

The independent judiciary

The most outstanding characteristic of the English judiciary is its independence from political or any other interests. In every court, the primary duty of a judge is to exercise discretion properly, and not prejudicially. In particular the judiciary must resist any improper pressure by the executive, by litigants, or by public opinion.

Tasks of the judge or magistrate

In court proceedings the judicial function requires the judge or magistrate to perform a number of tasks. He or she must:

(a) preside over the proceedings
(b) keep order in the courtroom
(c) rule on questions of fact, evidence and law
(d) make decisions
(e) give reasons for their decisions

The judicial function is indeed a multi-faceted one.

The judicial oath

As already discussed in Chapter 3, the role of the judge is to interpret the law. However, the judiciary is a statutory regulated body and is therefore expected to be impartial and independent. Here are the words of the judicial oath taken by all judges and magistrates:

> 'I do swear by Almighty God that I will well and truly serve our Sovereign . . . and I will do right to all manner of people after the laws and usages of this realm without fear or favour, affection or ill will . . . '

Upon the judiciary depends either the quality or weakness of the English legal system – and it is upon them we too depend to protect our rights and freedoms.

Tutorial

Practice questions

The following questions will help you revise and learn about the English judiciary and law officers:

1. Briefly explain how the involvement of both lay and professional members contributes to the work of the English judiciary.

2. List three of the senior judicial offices in the English legal system. Describe the functions of each.

3. Explain how the senior members of the judiciary are appointed.

4. Critically evaluate the role of the law officers within the English legal system.

5. Assess Professor Griffith's critique of the current judiciary – does it still apply? Do you agree with Griffith's conclusions, and why?

If you are not sure how to answer any of these questions, spend a few minutes reading this chapter again.

Seminar discussion
1. How important do you consider the use of ritual and hierarchy to the successful operation of the British judicial system?

2. Should there be more, or less, political input to the management of the judiciary?

Practical assignment
Visit a local magistrate's court, and make some brief notes on the conduct of the proceedings, and the various stages involved.

Further reading
Bailey & Gunn, *The Modern English Legal System* (3ed.), (1997), Sweet & Maxwell.
Pannick, *The Judges* (1996), OUP.
Griffiths, *The Politics of the Judiciary* (1996), Penguin.
Rozenberg, *In Search of Justice* (1996), Hodder & Stoughton.

8

The Role and Work of Tribunals

One minute summary – Tribunals of some description have been in existence since the eighteenth century, either as an extra-judicial or quasi-judicial form of court. Following the Franks Report of 1957, tribunals and enquiries have expanded into many public spheres and offer much to aggrieved citizens seeking redress for their complaints. The work of tribunals in the English legal system plays an ever increasing role in adjudication in our complex society. In this chapter we will see how tribunals first came about, their composition and types of work, and critically evaluate their effectiveness as a system of adjudication. The chapter will cover:

► how tribunals began
► tribunals and courts
► composition of tribunals
► statutory tribunals
► tribunals compared with courts
► tribunal procedures
► inquiries

How tribunals began

In 1957, the Franks Committee under Sir Oliver Franks reported on the growth of tribunals and inquiries. As a result there was enacted the 1958 Tribunal and Inquiries Act, later amended in 1971 and 1992. A Council on Tribunals was set up to oversee the workings of the various tribunals, in particular their composition, rules, purposes and remits. In contrast to the courts, tribunals are:

(a) free
(b) informal

More significantly, post-Franks, there was an expansion in the number of tribunals, and the range of work they covered. These tribunals commonly determine legal disputes between the citizen and the state. The disputes largely involve social issues ranging from housing to criminal injuries, social security benefits, immigration, education and employment.

Under various Acts of Parliament many new tribunals have been set up. They rule on the operation of schemes established under those Acts, and provide an alternative to the expensive and much slower traditional courts system. Since 1945 there have been more and more cases involving conflicts between an increasingly interventionist welfare state, its powerful functionaries, and the rights of private citizens. Today, there are at least sixty types of administrative tribunal, and there may well be hundreds of individual tribunals within each type operating locally.

Tribunals and courts

The Franks Committee (1957) established the need for an alternative method of adjudication, other than the courts, to rule on specialised matters. Many commentators have opposed the use of such tribunals, on the grounds that they do not have the same real legal authority as the courts. In fact, the tribunals are acting in a judicial capacity.

Much debate has surrounded the huge growth of tribunals within our legal system, and whether they should be regarded as part of the legal system. These concerns arise from the statement made in the Franks Report:

'Tribunals are not ordinary courts...We consider that tribunals should properly be regarded as machinery provided by parliament for adjudication rather than as part of the machinery of administration.'

Such a statement clearly sets out the purpose of tribunals as independent adjudication bodies. Once an Act of Parliament has created a particular tribunal for redress, the primary aim of that tribunal is to resolve legal disputes between aggrieved parties, whether between an individual and the state, or between two or more individuals.

Composition of tribunals

The 1992 Tribunals and Inquiries Act makes provision for the composition of tribunals. Most notably, it requires the chairperson to be legally qualified, except in special circumstances, such as in the Lands Tribunals where a surveyor is required.

Tribunals are usually composed of three members. Of these only one – the chair – is expected to be legally qualified. The other two are lay representatives. The lay persons are appointed locally, to reflect the local communities in which the adjudication takes place. A common feature of the English tribunal system is that it is regionally, therefore locally, organised. Yet it is managed under a national framework to ensure consistency and coherency, despite emergent local practices or idiosyncrasies.

The role of the 'wing'-members is to find the facts and adjudicate on the matters before them. The role of the chair is to guide procedures and advise the wing-members on points of law. The chairperson does not have a casting vote. Therefore, the wing-members can outvote the legally qualified chair in some cases.

A lot of training is given to tribunal chairs and members alike. Each specific type of tribunal is required by the Judicial Studies Board to undergo training. Such exercises include an update on the latest legislative developments and mock tribunal hearings, as well as induction and refresher courses.

Statutory tribunals

Some tribunals have considerable power in their particular areas of operation. Below is a list of the principal tribunals presently in existence:

Employment (formerly Industrial) Tribunals (ET)

These were established in 1964 as Industrial Tribunals. They are now governed by the Industrial Tribunals Act 1996, Employment Rights Act 1996, Employment Relations Act 1999, and by the Resolution of Employment Disputes Act 1998. These Acts set out their composition, major areas of competence, procedures and conciliation mechanisms. Their principal work is to hear claims of unfair dismissal, redundancy and discrimination (sex, race and disability) and to resolve disputes between employers and employees, and occasionally trades unions. In these tribunals, the legally-qualified chair is assisted by a representative from both a trade union and an employer's representative.

Social Security Appeal Tribunal (SSAT)

Social security tribunals were one of the first to be established. They were originally national insurance local tribunals, and supplementary benefit appeal tribunals. The 1998 Social Security Act now delegates the task of adjudicating on social security legislation to SSATs. The function of the social security tribunals is to make sure that the discretion to award social security benefits is not abused and that the aims of the legislation are being met.

Mental Health Review Tribunals (MHRT)

These operate under the Mental Health Act 1983. Such tribunals have wide powers to decide whether individuals should be detained for the purposes of compulsory treatment on the grounds of mental illness or disorder.

Immigration Appeal Tribunals (IAT)

IATs operate under the provisions of the various Immigration Acts and Regulations. These include the British Nationality Act 1981, Immigration Act 1992 and the Asylum and Immigration Act 1996. IATs have wide powers to decide whether individuals should be allowed to enter and/or remain within the UK. Unlike other tribunals, these appellate bodies are comprised of an adjudicator.

Medical Appeal and Disability Appeal Tribunals (MAT, DAT)

Formerly these operated independently from SSATs. They were composed of two medical practitioners and a chairperson, or in the case of disability appeals one medical practitioner and a disabled person. Subject to the provisions of the 1998 Social Security Act, these tribunals are merged into one under the remit of the SSAT (see above).

Residential Homes Tribunals (RHT)

This *ad hoc* tribunal is established under the 1984 Registered Homes Act. Its function is to hear appeals concerning the registration of residential care homes, nursing homes, and children's homes.

Lands Tribunal (LT)

Established under the Lands Tribunal Act 1949, its essential function is to determine the legality of, and the levels of compensation in relation to, compulsory purchase orders over land. It also considers matters relating to planning applications.

Rent Assessment Committee (RAC)

This tribunal deals with matters specifically relating to the rent charged for property. It resolves disputes between landlords and tenants of private accommodation, hears appeals from decisions of rent officers, and has the powers to fix rent in relation to furnished and unfurnished residential tenancies.

Child Support Appeal Tribunals (CSAT)

Under the Child Support Act 1991, provision is made for the determination of appeals from persons relating to the calculation of and orders to pay child support.

Other tribunals

Other tribunals include ones for pensions appeals, vaccine damage, education appeals, special educational needs, independent schools, national health service, agricultural land, Director of Fair Trading, copyright, transport, civil aviation, valuation, foreign compensation, VAT, income and corporation tax, and betting levy.

Notable omissions

Two notable omissions from the tribunal system are the:

1. *Criminal Injuries Board (CIB)* – This grants ex gratia payments to victims of violent crimes.

2. *Housing Benefit/ Council Tax Tribunal* (HBT/CTBT) – This hears claimants' appeals for rent or council tax rebates or allowances.

The reason is that they were established by royal prerogative and statutory regulations respectively, not by an Act of Parliament.

Tribunals compared with courts

Advantages over courts
The main advantages of tribunals over courts are:

(a) *Speed*. Courts can take as long as up to three years for your case to be heard. The median is one year. A tribunal hearing can take place within three to six months.

(b) *Cost*. To start proceedings in a court of law, a summonses or writ has to be issued. This piece of paper costs money. To initiate an appeal before a tribunal, no cost is involved. All that is required is the completion of the requisite form requesting an appeal. For example, in employment cases, an ET1 form (formerly an IT1) is completed by the aggrieved applicant employee.

(c) *Informality*. The Franks Committee argued that the most important value of a tribunal was its informality. No legal dress, no modes of address, and no rules of evidence should apply. In fact, everyday language should be used, and legal language should be avoided at all times, so that all the parties understand what is happening. Consequently, tribunals meet in a normal office-like building and room, and all the parties to the appeal sit around a table, rather than in a court-room setting. *Note*: A word of caution is required here, as such informality depends upon many factors, for example who is chairing the tribunal. Some chairpersons of tribunals are very judge-like (some in fact are judges) and tend to conduct the appeal hearing as if they were in a court, contrary to the ethos of the tribunal system. The lay members should be able to control this and act as a catalyst for informality.

(d) *Expertise*. Given their composition, tribunals are expected to be expert adjudication bodies. The inclusion of lay members provides valuable local knowledge.

(e) *Accessibility*. The fact that tribunals are regionally organised makes them very accessible, though most courts are locally administered too. More significantly, they are more accessible in how their appeal proceedings are begun. This is a straightforward matter, and does not involve a formal legal application for leave to appeal as in the courts.

(f) *Privacy*. Unlike courts of law, which are in the public domain, tribunals sit in private. Some tribunals do afford a right of public access, but few members of the public ever attend. The parties to a dispute can normally air their views in private.

Weaknesses compared with courts
In addition to these general strong points there are some key weaknesses in the system of tribunal adjudication:

1. *Appeals procedures*. Once the first tier of appeal is exhausted the appellants still have to resort to the courts on further appeal. This costs both money and time, and somewhat takes away from the tribunal system as a recourse for redress. Appeals at second tier stage become very legalistic.

2. *Publicity*. Whilst tribunals sit in private, there is generally no reason why the proceedings should not be reported in the local press. Whether the press are present or not, there is nothing to stop either party from reporting the proceedings themselves. The fact that tribunals sit locally often creates fear amongst the parties to an appeal, since they wonder whether matters of local interest will be publicised. For instance, each party to the appeal will receive a written decision.

3. *The provision of legal aid*. There is no provision for legal aid before tribunals. Consequently, most appellants are unrepresented and feel disadvantaged when confronted by a government department, or other major organisation. Research by Genn & Genn highlights that the levels of representation are very low before tribunals. However, they also demonstrate that being represented makes no real difference to the outcome, since over fifty percent of appeals succeed, irrespective of representation. Nevertheless, the fact that you have to appear in person before a

quasi-legal body often deters private citizens from using tribunals.

Tribunal procedures

Different tribunals adopt varying procedures for their sittings, but the main guiding principle is informality. The procedures to be followed depend upon the type of tribunal. For example, in an employment tribunal, the employer in a case of unfair dismissal will outline his reasons for dismissal; the dismissed employee will then respond.

1. Generally, before any tribunal each party is allowed to put their case.

2. During their evidence, whether written or oral, or with or without statements and/or witnesses, each party is allowed to ask the other questions.

3. The parties are also questioned by the tribunal.

4. Each party is then allowed to summarise their case.

5. Then, the tribunal retires to reach its determination in private. The tribunal returns and gives its decision, providing a written decision and reasons if requested.

Each type of tribunal has its own guidance on proceedings. These general rules, however, are intended to provide, according to Franks, 'a general framework for procedural fairness'.

Rules of evidence

There remains one key difference between courts and tribunals: the tribunals do not strictly apply the rules of evidence, as the courts do. For example, when tribunals adjudicate on facts, they can accept hearsay evidence, if they find it compelling. In a court of law, hearsay evidence is not admissible.

The standard of proof

Tribunals have one thing in common with the courts, that is the standard of proof required. As in the courts, a burden to prove their case is placed upon one of the parties. For instance, in a criminal matter before the courts, the burden of proof lies on the prosecution to prove 'beyond reasonable doubt' that the defendant is guilty. Similarly, before a social security tribunal, the standard of proof lies on the Department of Social Security to argue that the claimant is not entitled to receive some form of social security benefit.

Representation before tribunals

There is no right as such to legal representation in English law. The principles of natural justice are supposed to ensure and safeguard a right to a fair hearing. Moreover, as noted above, due to the absence of legal aid for tribunal hearings, little representation occurs.

However, research by Genn & Genn found that some representation did take place. This was largely free representation. It was provided for example by a local Citizen's Advice Bureau, law centre, a legal charity such as the Free Representation Unit and Child Poverty Action Group, unions, or some other advocacy group or organisation. For example, the Royal British Legion is most active in Pensions Appeal Tribunal hearings.

Unlike courts of law, representatives before tribunals do not have to be legally qualified. In the courts the concept of 'McKenzie's friend' exists, whereby an unqualified person can speak for the person. In tribunals a lay representative can address the tribunal and represent his/her friend or client. Generally, very few lawyers appear before tribunals, unless their client is prepared to pay. In any event, the unrepresented appellant should be helped by the tribunal to state their case as best they can. Normally this duty lies upon the chair of the tribunal.

Cost of tribunals

As noted above, tribunals cost nothing to the parties. They are a free service, funded by the taxpayer. However, should the appellant's case in certain tribunals be found to be 'frivolous or vexatious' the fear of costs may – in very exceptional cases – loom large.

Publicity and public proceedings

Whilst a tribunal may sit in private, it is still a public adjudication body. As such, its proceedings are recorded by the tribunal and the records kept by the appropriate tribunal office.

Some tribunals do have to power to order reporting restrictions. This can safeguard the anonymity of the parties. However, this is used only in exceptional cases.

Appeals

Appeals from tribunal decisions vary according to the particular type of tribunal. For example:

(a) An appeal from a decision of the SSAT lies to the Social Security Commissioners.

(b) An appeal from an ET will go before the Employment Appeal tribunal (EAT).

These second tier appellate bodies are often established by statute. In any event, appeal often lies to the High Court or the Civil Division of the Court of Appeal on questions of fact, law, or evidence. The leave of either court is necessary. Enormous legal costs start being incurred at this point, as the more formal legal framework of the courts replaces the characteristically informal and free or cheap ethos of the tribunal.

Inquiries

Another common feature of modern adjudication is the use of the **statutory inquiry**. Such public inquiries are set up on an *ad hoc* basis, according to the perceived need. Generally they are launched in response to some major disaster or public controversy. They are usually chaired by a High Court judge or more senior member of the judiciary.

More often than not, an inquiry team is set up to assist the chair.

Normally this is drawn from among both local people and experts in the subject under examination. In this role, the judge and the inquiry team act as fact finders. Many of these inquiries concern politically sensitive issues. It is therefore imperative that the members of an inquiry remain independent from any external pressures or publicity.

Some recent public inquiries

Here is a list of recent inquiries:

(a) The Red Lion Square riots (Lord Scarman)
(b) The Bradford City disaster (Lord Taylor)
(c) The Hillsborough football stadium fire (Popplewell J)
(d) Arms to Iraq (Scott LJ)
(e) Standards in public life (Lord Nolan, later Lord Neill)
(f) The Dunblane shootings (Lord Cullen)
(g) BSE in cattle (Sir Nicholas Phillips)
(h) Lawrence Inquiry (Death of Stephen Lawrence) (Sir William Macpherson)

Tutorial

Practice questions

The following questions will help you revise and learn about the role and work of tribunals:

1. Describe how and why tribunals were established in the UK. Summarise their relevance and value in modern society.

2. List the principal tribunals which exist in the English legal system and analyse their functions.

3. Consider the effectiveness of the English tribunal system. What are (a) its main strengths and (b) its main weaknesses?

4. 'According to research by Genn & Genn, being represented before a tribunal makes little difference to the outcome'. Critically evaluate this statement in view of the general aims and procedures of tribunals.

If you are not sure how to answer any of these questions, then spend a few minutes reading this chapter again.

Seminar discussion
Modern society is changing fast in so many ways – single households, working from home, the internet, genetic discoveries and applications. Is there some aspect of contemporary life where you think a new type of tribunal is needed?

Student assignment
Choose a particular type of tribunal, contact its nearest offices, and enquire as to whether you could attend to observe some forthcoming proceedings in action. Explain that you are a law student.

Further reading
Franks Report (1957), *Committee on Administrative Tribunals and Inquiries*, HMSO.
Annual Report of the Council on Tribunals, 1997-98, HMSO.
Bailey & Gunn, *The Modern English Legal System* (3ed.), (1997), Sweet & Maxwell.
Genn & Genn, *The Effectiveness of Representation before Tribunals* (1989), LCD Research, HMSO.

9

Ombudspersons

One minute summary – An ombudsperson is an official to whom complaints or grievances can be addressed. The word is Swedish in origin and means 'representative of the people'. Other Scandinavian countries such as Finland and Norway have similar officials, as do Denmark and New Zealand. Following this international model, the UK adopted its first ombudsman in 1967. In this chapter we examine the different methods of alternative dispute resolution which are available to the citizen without going to court. You will explore the ombudsmen mechanism, the legislative framework, the growth of public services ombudsmen, and the impact of mediation, conciliation and arbitration on complaints procedures. The chapter covers:

▶ the ombudsman system
▶ public management
▶ an evaluation of the ombudsman system
▶ mediation
▶ conciliation
▶ arbitration
▶ the small claims procedure in the county court

The ombudsman system

The first ombudsman was introduced in the UK following the Whyatt Report of 1961. In the thirty years since its introduction there has been immense growth in this type of scheme in both the public and private spheres. We will explain each of these below:

The legislative framework
The position of the first ombudsman was established by The

Parliamentary Commissioner Act 1967. It provides that complainants are entitled to pursue their complaints with the ombudsman so long as they have exhausted all complaints procedures provided by the body complained of (eg DSS, NHS, etc). Such a prohibition is subject to the discretion of the ombudsman who tends to interpret it in favour of the complainant. Further Acts of Parliament enacted other ombudspeople, as listed below. Today there is vast legislative framework in English law covering complaint handling, investigation and resolution outside the courts system.

The various ombudspeople

The original concept of the ombudsman is Scandinavian. The function of the office-holder is to investigate complaints of **maladministration**. This exists where the performance of a government department, local authority, European institution, or other public service has fallen below an acceptable standard.

▶ *The Parliamentary Ombudsperson* – The Parliamentary Commissioner for Administration (PCA) was established under the 1967 Parliamentary Commissioner Act. The office seeks to redress any maladministration proved to have been suffered by members of the public. **Maladministration** is defined as consisting of *'neglect, bias, delay, incompetence, arbitrariness, perversity and turpitude'*. This list is known as the Crossman catalogue, and is named after Richard Crossman, the Labour Minister who introduced the ombudsman. Citizens who feel aggrieved by the actions or omissions of any government department can complain to their MP, requesting that she/he passes their complaint onto the PCA for investigation. Having investigated the matter, the PCA issues a report and makes any necessary recommendations. The PCA cannot provide a direct remedy, but can recommend one. Under s.12(3) of the Parliamentary Commissioner Act 1967 the PCA is expressly precluded from questioning the merits of particular decisions taken in the absence of maladministration.

▶ *The Local Government Ombudsman* – This office has existed since 1972 under the Local Government Act. This official may investigate complaints concerning local authority services. In contrast to the PCA and HSC, members of the public can complain directly to the local government ombudsmen. Moreover, the local government ombudsmen system operates on a regional basis. There are eight in all in the UK. They deal with complaints relating to housing, education, social services and other services provided by local authorities.

▶ *The Health Ombudsperson* – The Health Services Commissioner (HSC) or 'ombudsman' fulfils a role formerly undertaken by the PCA. The office was set up in 1993. This grievance body was separated from the work of the PCA and given its own office by Act of Parliament (see the Health Services Commissioner Act 1993). This was necessary because of the growth in workload relating to NHS complaints alone. Like the PCA, the HSC investigates health service provision, issuing reports and making recommendations to the Department of Health.

▶ *The European Ombudsperson* – The European ombudsperson is a relatively new appointment. It was introduced under the 1992 Treaty on European Union. Its office-holder is appointed by the European Parliament. He or she may be removed from office for misconduct by the European Court of Justice at the request of the European parliament. This ombudsperson is completely independent in the exercise of official duties. EU citizens have a right, by way of direct access, to complain to the EU ombudsperson about the activities of the institutions of the EU. Where a finding of maladministration is recorded, it is referred to the offending institution, which has three months in which to respond. The EU ombudsperson submits an annual report to the European parliament. The only exclusion from the remit of the EU ombudsman is the work of the European Court of Justice, that being of a judicial nature and not administration.

Public management

In the 1990s, under a new regime of public management, several ombudspersons were introduced, relevant to various service provisions. The advent of well-defined charters of standards of services, and quality of delivery, now require the establishment of various complaints and regulatory bodies. From its historical beginnings, the ombudsman scheme has expanded greatly in order to become a system rather than just a person. The general public is now well accustomed to turning to an ombudsperson when experiencing problems with the service they are using.

Public services
With the growth of public services and the expansion of the ombudsperson scheme, various public service providers have set up their own ombudspeople. Examples include:

    legal services
    building societies
    prisons
    pensions
    banking
    insurance

These ombudsmen have the same powers of investigation as the PCA though, unlike the PCA, they have the power to order remedies. The banking ombudsman, for instance, can award financial compensation.

Watchdogs
Just as the public sector service providers set up ombudsmen, so the private sector at the same time established watchdogs. Examples include OFGAS, OFWAT, and OFTEL. They deal with complaints about gas, water and telecommunications services respectively. Similar in their roles to ombudsmen, these watchdogs handle customer complaints and can rectify errors and award compensation.

An evaluation of the ombudspeople system

The ombudsman scheme has often been criticised. Criticism has grown along with greater access and public awareness of the scheme. The counter argument to criticism is that the workload – of the PCA in particular – is rising. There were some 1,933 cases in 1996, compared to just 500 in 1986. High profile investigations by the ombudsman, such as the PCA in the Barlow Clowes affair, have raises the public's awareness of the scheme, and the demand for its services.

The most serious weakness of the scheme is its failure to provide a definitive remedy. Most of all, the official can only report and make a recommendation to the body found to have acted badly. The organisation 'Justice' and the National Consumer Council have both argued strongly for reform of the system to rectify these weaknesses. It is therefore proposed to widen the powers of the ombudsmen to include the power to award appropriate remedies and to investigate matters beyond 'maladministration' as originally defined.

Mediation

An alternative to the ombudsman scheme is mediation. Mediation is the process in which a third party acts as a conduit through which two disputing parties communicate in an attempt to resolve a problem. The mediator can move between the parties, and communicate their opinions without the parties having to come face to face. Or, the mediator can operate with the parties present. Either way, the emphasis is on the parties themselves working out an agreement to settle their dispute.

Mediation in divorce

Mediation has a key part to play in family matters and personal relationships. Here, the adversarial approach of the traditional legal system has tended to aggravate the differences between individuals. This has not helped to bring about amicable settlements. In divorce cases, mediation has therefore been used to help the parties themselves to work out a settlement outside the courts.

The Family Law Act 1996 has introduced the concept of a 'no fault' divorce. It has abolished the old grounds of divorce of adultery and unreasonable behaviour, but couples will have to wait at least 12 months before their divorce is confirmed. Instead of filing a divorce petition, the person wanting a divorce simply has to submit a statement certifying that the marriage has broken down.

The divorce process now requires the parties to attend an informal meeting three months before they make their statement of marital breakdown. They then have to wait a further nine months for their divorce. During this time they should

(a) reflect on whether the marriage could be saved
(b) have an opportunity for reconciliation
(c) consider arrangements relating to finance, property and children

The 1996 Act encourages the use of mediation in appropriate cases. After receiving a statement of marital breakdown, the court may direct the parties to attend a meeting with a mediator to have the mediation process explained to them. The role of the mediator is restricted to sorting out aspects of the divorce relating to finance and children. The mediator should refer the case to an appropriate counsellor if it appears that the parties to the marriage might be open to reconciliation.

Conciliation

Conciliation takes mediation a step further. It gives the mediator the power to suggest grounds for compromise and a possible basis for conclusive agreement. Both mediation and conciliation have been available for industrial disputes under the government-funded Advisory Conciliation and Arbitration Service. One of the statutory functions of ACAS is to try to resolve industrial disputes by discussion and negotiation. If the parties agree, the Service can take a more active part as arbitrator in a particular dispute.

Conciliation in employment disputes

Under the 1998 Resolution of Employment Disputes Act, the powers and role of ACAS have been extended in an attempt to resolve disputes between employers and employees. Before the 1998 Act, ACAS settlements were a voluntary matter between employers and employees. In fact conciliation or mutual settlement – the COT3 procedure as it was known – became part and parcel of the pre-tribunal hearing process.

However, under the 1998 Act, employees in dispute with their employers will be allocated a conciliator. Meetings between all parties will be convened, with the aim of settling the disputes. Conciliation has become therefore mandatory, since efforts to conciliate must now be reported to the Employment Tribunal.

Arbitration

Arbitration is the procedure in which disputing parties refer the issue to a third party for resolution, rather than take the case at great expense to the ordinary law courts. In employment, industrial disputes arbitration featured quite dramatically in the UK in the 1960s and 1970s. An institution known as the Central Arbitration Committee, for instance, was established in order to resolve any industrial strife.

Arbitration is used widely, quite aside from employment matters. In the county courts, for example, arbitration hearings are commonplace.

Arbitration procedure

The arbitration procedure is governed by the Arbitration Acts (AA) 1950 and 1979. Arbitration is treated under s.6 of the AA 1950 as a reference to a single arbitrator. The AA 1950 and 1979 provide that the procedure must be carried out in a 'judicial manner', in line with natural justice. At the conclusion of the hearing the arbitrator is required to provide reasons for any award given.

Relationship to ordinary courts

Arbitration proceedings are open to challenge through judicial review, on the grounds that they were not conducted in a judicial manner. The AA 1950 allowed either party to the proceedings to have questions of law authoritatively determined by the High Court through the procedure of 'case stated'. The High Court could also set aside the decision of the arbitrator on grounds of fact, law, or procedure. The arbitration process was supposed to provide a quick and relatively cheap method of deciding disputes, but the appeals procedures meant that parties could delay the final decision and in so doing increase the costs.

The AA 1979 abolished the 'case stated' procedure and curtailed the right to appeal. The findings of the arbitrator as to questions of fact are now conclusive and cannot be appealed against.

Advantages of arbitration

There are numerous advantages to be gained from using arbitration rather than the court system:

(a) *privacy* – the hearings are held in private, or 'in chambers' as it is termed.

(b) *informality* – the proceedings are informal. The arbitrator acts as an umpire and independent third party.

(c) *speed* – arbitration hearings tend to be short and frequent. It is common to make three or more attempts at arbitration before having recourse to law.

(d) *cost* – the only costs are the fees of the arbitrator. These are usually at a fixed rate and set and agreed before the arbitration commences.

(e) *expertise* – the arbitrator is normally an expert in the field. More usually he is a registered, therefore fully qualified, arbitrator.

Small claims procedure in the county court

Since 1973 an arbitration service has been available in the county court specifically for the settlement of relatively small claims. Since

1995, reference to arbitration is normally automatic in cases involving sums of money up to £3,000. Arbitration proceedings may be used in situations involving more than £3,000 where the parties concerned agree. The limit with regard to personal injury cases remains at £1,000. The Woolf Reforms, in force since April 1999, have extended this facility. See chapter 4 for a fuller discussion.

Procedure

Arbitration proceedings begin with an individual filing a 'statement of claim' at the county court. Once this statement has been received by the court, and a 'defence' filed by the respondent, the district judge sets a date for a directions hearing. At this hearing the judge ascertains the facts from each party and enquires as to whether the matter can be settled. If not, a date for trial is set. In any event, the loser in small claims hearings will not have to pay the winner's costs. Each party bears their own costs.

Tutorial

Practice questions

The following questions will help you revise and learn about the function and powers of the ombudsmen:

1. Summarise and compare the main methods of dispute resolution available under English law.

2. Briefly summarise the impact of the ombudsmen system on the English legal system.

3. Provide six examples of the various ombudsmen and their services.

4. Explain the difference between mediation and conciliation.

5. When might it be better to seek arbitration rather than go to court?

If you are not sure how to answer any of these questions, then spend a few minutes reading this chapter again.

Seminar discussion
'Alternative methods of dispute resolution are quicker, cheaper and more effective than the courts'. How far do you think this is true?

Student assignment
Select one of the ombudsmen services, and use the internet to discover how well or otherwise it offers its services to the public online.

Further reading
Parliamentary Commissioner Acts 1967 and 1994, HMSO.
Justice Report, *Our Fettered Ombudsman* (1977), HMSO.
Justice-All Souls Review, 'Administrative Law Reforms' (1988), HMSO.
Harlow & Rawlings, *Law & Administration* (1984) Weidenfeld & Nicolson.

10

The Cost and Realities of Going to Law

One minute summary – The legal aid system was introduced by the Labour government after the second world war (1939-45) to allow low income and poorer people to have access to the justice system. Before, such people had to rely on charity if they went to court, or their own financial resources and capital. The funding of legal services has always been controversial. In this final chapter we will explore the cost of going to law. We will examine the legal aid system, and forms of legal aid and franchising. We will also analyse the realities of resorting to law to resolve legal disputes, including where to obtain advice and representation. Lastly, we will consider future reforms to the funding of the English legal system. The chapter covers:

▶ funding the English legal system
▶ legal aid
▶ legal franchising
▶ free legal advice
▶ other models of funding
▶ conditional fee arrangements
▶ future reforms

Funding the English legal system

Resorting to litigation to resolve disputes costs a great deal of money and time. Indeed, the costs of litigation can be quite phenomenal. The funding of the English legal system has two major sources:

(a) government funding, paid for by the taxpayer
(b) individual litigant's resources, which can include their own savings, or insurance policies.

Whatever method is chosen, both give rise to the central question about access to law: does the cost prevent people obtaining the 'justice' to which they are entitled (ie the right to defend or bring proceedings)? The unquantifiable and no doubt steep costs of going to law deter many potential litigants from even contemplating going to court.

In recent years the question of the cost of going to law has become more significant. In 1997 the Lord Chancellor was challenged in litigation for raising court fees. In the Witham case (see R v. Lord Chancellor ex p Witham (1997) 13 March, *The Times*), the High Court determined that the Lord Chancellor's raising of court fees did prevent persons from bringing their cases before the courts, in particular those persons on low incomes or benefits. Subsequently their Lordships (Rose LJ and Laws J) found that access to the courts was a constitutional right and therefore the Lord Chancellor's act was unlawful. As a result, the Lord Chancellor's order to raise court fees was quashed. Going to law may be a fundamental human right, but in reality it can cost people or organisations a great deal of money.

Legal aid

As the cost of litigation has grown, so since 1972 has legal aid. Legal aid is granted to individual persons according to the merits of the case they intend to bring, and according to their financial means. Legal aid seeks to assist those with limited financial means.

Legal aid is administered by the Legal Aid Board. The duty of the Board is to ensure that the best price is achieved for quality services to meet an individual person's requirements for legal advice and assistance. Another role of the Board is to issue and enforce its code of practice.

The legal aid framework covers many different legal services (green form, civil, criminal and ABWOR) and law practices nationwide. The general requirements relating to eligibility for legal aid are reviewed annually.

Types of legal aid

The term 'legal aid' is used to cover a wide range of subsidised or free services. Strictly speaking however it only refers to one sort of help: representation in court. Legal advice and assistance (also known as the **green form** scheme) covers advice and help with any legal problem; and, in some cases, under what is called **assistance by way of representation** (ABWOR), it also covers going to court. Civil legal aid is available for cases where advice or letter-writing has not solved a problem and the matter has to go to court. Under the 'green form' scheme, a solicitor can undertake ordinary legal work up to an initial limit of two hours' worth of work for a client who passes the relevant means test.

Civil legal aid

Since 1989, civil legal aid has been administered by the Legal Aid Board. To obtain legal aid an applicant must satisfy two tests:

(a) the **merits** test – a person must show the Board that he or she has reasonable grounds for taking, defending or being party to an action.

(b) the **means** test – the person should not have capital and income of £3,000 and above.

In civil matters, legal aid can be given for pursuing contractual, property, tortious and/or personal injury claims. However, a person can be refused legal aid if it appears to the Board unreasonable to grant representation.

Criminal legal aid

The decision as to whether to grant legal aid is made by the court clerk according to criteria in the Legal Aid Act 1988. These criteria cover the merits of the case, as well as the defendant's right to representation in criminal matters, and his/her means. The same capital restrictions exist as for civil legal aid, but the income limit is £50 per week. In criminal legal aid, in particular, legally-aided funded defendants may be asked to make some contribution towards their funding, dependant on their income. The only exception is where the defendant is receiving social security benefits. In such cases, no contribution will be expected.

Criminal legal aid often covers use of the **duty solicitor** scheme.

A defendant who is unrepresented, and does not have a solicitor, can on arrest at the police station or at court seek the assistance of a volunteer lawyer. This duty solicitor will represent and/or advise the defendant free of charge. Duty solicitors work according to a voluntary rota.

Legal franchising

In October 1993, following a pilot scheme in the Birmingham area, solicitors who meet certain management criteria will have devolved to them certain powers previously exercised by the Legal Aid Board. This is intended to reduce the administrative costs to the Board. In return for meeting efficiency criteria, the law practices will receive financial benefits such as a lump-sum payment from the Legal Aid Board, on account, as soon as a case is approved.

Consequently, since 1994, some legal aid services have been provided under contracts, known as franchises, between the Legal Aid Board and various law firms. Under this franchising, the Legal Aid Board delegates its powers to award legal aid to the individual law practices concerned.

Free legal advice

All kinds of organisations and statutory bodies, such as the National Consumer Council, provide information and advice on rights. Since the 1970s a host of voluntary advice agencies has emerged, such as the Citizens Advice Bureau (CABx), who also provide free advice. It often falls upon many of these organised free centres to advise, and in some cases assist, those who are less well off. Examples of organisations where free legal advice can be obtained are considered below:

Law centres
There are 52 law centres in England and Wales. They are staffed by salaried solicitors, articled clerks and non-lawyer experts. They are funded by local and central government, and charitable

organisations. They have 'shop front' access and aim to be user-friendly and non-intimidating. They are managed by committees and represented nationally by the Law Centres Federation.

Law centres advise persons on most legal subjects, though some do specialise for example in debts, housing or immigration. This specialisation depends upon their location and the needs of the local community which they serve. Law centres take on individual cases, providing, for example, advice on landlord and tenant matters and representing people at tribunals. Some centres also take on group work since quite often the problems of one client are part of a wider problem.

Citizens Advice Bureaux

The Citizens Advice Bureaux (CABx) is the largest, national advisory organisation in the UK. Funded by local authorities, administered by management committees and run by volunteers, the bureaux provide advice and information on almost any issue. The founding principles of the CABx are that they are: free, independent, confidential and non-judgemental. Some CABx provide representation in both the courts and certain tribunals.

The CABx offer a localised service, organised regionally, but supported and represented nationally by the National Association of Citizens Advice Bureaux (NACAB), whose head office is in London. NACAB represents CABx interests, lobbies, arranges for the training of volunteers and undertakes large-scale social research, based on data collected by its local CABx.

Other organisations and charities

Other organisations can provide free information and advice. They include trade unions, charities, churches, and community projects. For example, some local authorities run welfare rights centres. Other emerging advice groups in the 1990s are neighbourhood and community centres, and young persons' advice centres. Many charities such as MENCAP, RNIB or RNID and the Terrence Higgins Trust provide advice to their members, mainly in their own specialist areas such as disability, education, unemployment, drugs, health or training – the list is endless. Evidently, within our modern society there are many excellent organisations able to provide support, advice and assistance to people in need.

Other models of funding

In 1979 the Royal Commission on Legal Services, chaired by Lord Benson, examined the funding of the English legal system. In particular, it reviewed legal aid. More recently, the newly elected Labour government of 1997 established a review under Sir Peter Middleton. Its intention was to see what legal aid was needed and how far society could afford to fund the legal system. In September 1998, the Middleton Review made its recommendations to the government. These included suggestions drawn from comparative studies about other models for the provision of legal services. Two of these models are discussed below:

The public defender system

The USA has historically contained a free legal service model within its legal tradition. This is most evident in its public defender system. The office of 'public defender' refers to a state funded lawyer appointed to represent those who cannot afford to pay for legal services. This model is much like the British duty solicitor scheme. In fact, the duty solicitor scheme appears to have been modelled on the US Public Defender's Office. However, unlike his British counterpart, the US lawyer can help people in all proceedings, not just in criminal matters.

Free legal services

Many European states operate free legal services. Resembling law centres and CABx in the UK, the 'free legal services' model is a fully state funded one. Under this model, the client makes a contribution or pays for his/her legal services, should they win their case and receive financial compensation. This model is very like the conditional fee system now in operation in the UK for personal injury litigation.

Conditional fee arrangements

Section 58 of the 1990 Courts and Legal Services Act permitted the Lord Chancellor to introduce conditional fee arrangements, though not in criminal cases, family cases or those involving children (s.58(10)). Conditional fees can be based on an 'uplift' from the level of fee the lawyer would normally charge for the sort of work in question.

The system came into effect in June 1995. Such agreements are legal, provided that they comply with any requirements imposed by the Lord Chancellor and are not 'contentious business agreements'.

Recent reforms

At the time of writing the government has recently enacted its Access to Justice Act. Following much consultation by the Lord Chancellor, this Act seeks to modernise the fifty year old legal aid system. It establishes a new Legal Services Commission to replace the Legal Aid Board. The Commission will be responsible both for community legal services and for the criminal defence services. The present system of legal aid is to be replaced by a:

(a) community legal services fund, for civil and family cases

(b) criminal defence services fund, which will replace the existing criminal legal aid provision

The biggest reform comes in the form of salaried defenders who will give advice and representation for free. Some of this free advice work will be contracted out to some defenders in local areas.

Controversially, the Lord Chancellor will receive much greater power to give directions to the Legal Services Commission. This runs counter to the current independent status of the current Legal Aid Board, and marks a departure from the Lord Chancellor's present role which is one of guidance only.

A contingency legal aid fund has been omitted from these

proposals. Clearly, the government does not foresee the full-scale introduction of contingency fees as a priority. As the legal aid system braces itself for change, the future from 27th July 1997 provides a new legal landscape, in terms of both legal representation and the costs of going to law.

Tutorial

Practice questions
The following questions will help you revise and learn about the cost of going to law:

1. What is legal aid? Explain and categorise the various types of legal aid and services are available.

2. Describe the current methods and models of funding the English legal system.

3. Briefly summarise the strengths and weaknesses of the current legal aid system

4. Analyse the impact which legal franchising and a contingency fee system might have on the funding of legal services in the UK.

5. Identify and assess the case for reform of the funding of legal services.

6. 'The rich man has a lawyer to advise him, whilst the poor resort to charity'. Examine this statement in view of the growth in free advice services and the forthcoming future reforms.

If you are not sure how to answer any of these questions, then spend a few minutes reading this chapter again.

Seminar discussion
1. Is there any long term way of cutting the costs of going to law?

2. Are there circumstances in which people should be financially discouraged from going to law?

Student assignment

A hotel manager aged 44, Mrs A tripped on a pavement, and suffered serious injuries which resulted in the loss of her job. She intends to sue the council for negligence and will not qualify for legal aid. Try to find out how much it might cost her to bring a strongly contested case to trial. Base your estimate on the hourly rates likely to be charged by her solicitor and barrister, and the number of hours of work required by each.

Further reading

Blair et al, *Law Reform for all* (1997), Blackstone Press.

Access to Justice Bill (1998), HMSO.

Legal Aid Board, *Legal Aid Guidance* (1997), HMSO.

Report on Legal Aid: 'Striking the Balance' (1996), HMSO.

CPAG Handbook on Legal Aid (1998), Child Poverty Action Group.

You made it to the end . . .

Good luck in your studies!

Web Sites for Law Students

The internet, or world wide web, is an amazingly useful resource, giving the student nearly free and almost immediate information on any topic. Ignore this vast and valuable store of materials at your peril! The following list of web sites may be helpful for you. Please note that neither the author nor the publisher is responsible for content or opinions expressed on the sites listed, which are simply intended to offer starting points for students. Also, please remember that the internet is a fast-evolving environment, and links may come and go. If you have some favourite sites you would like to see mentioned in future editions of this book, please write to Stephen Hardy, c/o Studymates (address on back cover) or email him at:

stephenhardy@studymates.co.uk.

You will find a free selection of useful and readymade student links for English law and other subjects at the Studymates web site. Happy surfing!

http://www.studymates.co.uk

College of Law
http://www.lawcol.org.uk
Provides a nationwide coverage for students with full-time courses available at its four branches in central London, Chester, Guildford and York.

The Court Service
http://www.courtservice.gov.uk/cs-home.htm
The Court Service is an executive agency of the Lord Chancellor's Department which provides administrative support to the courts and tribunals within the UK.

Commission for Racial Equality
http://www.open.gov.uk/cre
The CRE promotes racial equality and anti-discriminatory practice on grounds of race within the United Kingdom.

Crown Prosecution Service
http://www.cps.gov.uk
The Crown Prosecution Service provides the main criminal prosecution services within the United Kingdom.

The Court of European Human Rights
http://www.dhcour.coe.fr/
The European Court of Human Rights enforces and interprets the rights of citizens held under the 1950 European Convention on Human Rights.

The Criminal Cases Review Commission
http://www.ccrc.gov.uk
The Criminal Cases Review Commission independently investigates any alleged miscarriages of justice.

Cyber Law Centre
http://www.cyberlawcentre.org.uk/
A useful collection of legal resources which includes relevant links, mailing lists and research tools, with more to come.

Equal Opportunities Commission
http://www.eoc.org.uk
The Equal Opportunities Commission is the expert body in Great Britain on equality between men and women.

European Institutions
http://www.europa.eu.int/
The European Institutions, the Commission, Court and Council and Parliament, administer and govern the workings and policies of the European Union.

General Council of the Bar
http://www.barcouncil.org.uk
Find out more about the Bar Council, the governing body of the English bar.

Hansard
http://www.parliament.the-stationery-office.co.uk/pa/cm/hansard.htm
Hansard is the daily verbatim reporting body of the proceedings in Parliament, including the judgements of the Judicial Committee of the House of Lords (see http://www.parliament.the-stationery-office.co.uk/pa/ld/ldjudinf.htm).

Her Majesty's Stationery Office
http://www.hmso.gov.uk
HMSO provides the publication of all official and government information, such as Acts of parliament, statutory instruments, EU documents, Bills before parliament, white and green papers and consultation documents.

Home Office
http://www.homeoffice.gov.uk
The Home Office is the government department responsible for internal affairs in England and Wales. Its main business is law and order, and includes the police, the prisons, and immigration matters.

Human Rights Web
http://www.hrweb.org
A valuable resource for information on human rights and civil liberties.

Inns of Court
http://www.online-law.co.uk/bar/inns_of_court.html
The Inns are described here with some interesting historical background and links to some of the chambers in each.

International Court of Justice
http://www.icj-cij.org/
The International Court of Justice at the Hague is the principal judicial organ of the United Nations.

Information for Lawyers
http://www.infolaw.co.uk
Information for Lawyers Limited is a gateway to the UK's legal internet. It contains monthly legal news, law associations' contacts, lawtech resources and law publishers, and lots more information on law services.

Judicial Studies Board
http://www.cix.co.uk/-jsb/
The Judicial Studies Board provides training and instruction for the English judiciary.

The Law Commission
http://www.gtnet.gov.uk/lawcomm/
The Law Commission is the statutory law reform body in the UK.

The Law Society
http://www.lawsoc.org.uk
The Law Society of England & Wales provides services and information to solicitors and legal practitioners throughout the UK and worldwide.

Law Society of Ireland
http://ireland.iol.ie/resource/lawsociety/

Law Society of Scotland
http://www.lawscot.org.uk

Legal Action Group
http://www.lag.org.uk
LAG is a national independent charity which campaigns for equal access to justice for all. It provides support to lawyers and advisers, and campaigns for improvements in the law.

Legal Aid Board
http://www.open.gov.uk/lab
The Legal Aid Board monitors the running of the legal aid scheme and supervises the legal aid franchise scheme.

Lord Chancellor's Department
http://www.open.gov.uk/lcd
The Lord Chancellor's Department is responsible for administering the English legal system. It is primarily responsible for the effective management of the courts, the appointment of judges, magistrates and other judicial office holders, the administration of legal aid, and overseas legislative reform.

National Association of Citizens Advice Bureaux
http://www.nacab.org.uk/
The national headquarters office.

Northern Circuit Commercial Bar Association
http://www.nccba.org.uk
Formed in 1996 to promote the work of barristers specialising in commercial law who centre their work on the north west of England.

The Ombudsman
http://www.ombudsman.org.uk
The Office of Parliamentary Commissioner for Administration exists to investigate complaints against government departments.

Prison Service
http://www.open.gov.uk/prison
Her Majesty's Prison Service serves the public by keeping in custody those committed by the courts, and generally organises and administers the British prison system.

Student Law Centre
http://www.studentlaw.com/sitemap
The Student Law Centre provides information on legal education, how to become a solicitor and barrister, legal updates, vacation placements, student links and the Legal 500.

Socio-Legal Studies Association
http://www.wmin.ac.uk/LLC/Law/slsawelc.html
The Social-Legal Studies Association is an international association of law teachers, practitioners and students. Its web site
provides information on the aims and activities of the association,
a newsletter and information on its members.

Student Law Centre
http://www.studentlaw.com/
Legalease's student site.

Youth Justice Board
http://www.youth-justice-board.gov.uk/
The Youth Justice Board for England and Wales is a new executive
non-departmental public body established in 1998 under the
Crime and Disorder Act 1998, to advise on the supervision and
administration of youth justice within England and Wales.

Appendix 1
Key core legal skills checklist

The following is a list of key legal skills. These valuable attributes will stand you in good stead, not only as a law student, but in the real world of work as a professional person.

The skills

1. Present a clearly written legal argument (*writing skills*).

2. Orally argue a coherently structured case (*advocacy skills*).

3. Comprehend, assess and evaluate a set of facts and apply the relevant law and advise persons on their rights and liabilities (*analytical skills*).

4. Extrapolate relevant, accurate and reliable information from people (*interpersonal/interviewing skills*).

5. Construct simple statements from complex information (*research skills*).

6. Able to effectively plan and organise time, and to share information/tasks with other people (*teamworking/negotiating skills*).

7. Attain competency in computing/electronic information systems (*IT skills*).

Check that you possess all of these key core skills, and have evidence to demonstrate each of them. Try rating yourself 1 to 10 for each, and identify those areas where you feel there is room for improvement.

Appendix 2
Check your overall progress

Once you have read this Studymate in full, you should be competent to discuss and write effectively about all the following topic areas. Tick off the ones you feel comfortable about so far.

❏ Legal terms, labels and studying law.

❏ Sources of English law.

❏ The courts system.

❏ The principles of statutory interpretation.

❏ Legislation.

❏ The law-making processes within the English and European legal systems.

❏ The impact of European law on English law and the English legal system.

❏ The branches of the legal profession.

❏ The English judiciary.

❏ The role and work of tribunals.

❏ The ombudspeople framework for the redress of grievances, and alternative dispute resolution mechanisms.

❏ The cost of going to law.

When you can tick off all these items, you will have gained a good understanding of the English legal system at work.

▶ *Tip* – If you still feel unsure about any of these areas, spend a few minutes re-reading the appropriate chapter.

Appendix 3
Preparing written work and answering examination questions

Writing legal opinions, advice, complex letters and legal documents is the business of lawyers. In just the same way, undertaking assignments forms part and parcel of every student's academic studies. Below is some general guidance on how to prepare successful written work and answer examination questions.

Assignments

The first stage in preparing for an assignment is to understand the question put. Having understood the aims of the question, you should then research the relevant legal subject area. Preparation therefore begins in the law library. Having done your research, you can now start to write your answer in draft form. Good presentation of written work will count very favourably towards your efforts, though good content will earn more marks.

Presentation of assignments
As for presentation, clarity of expression is vital. Get into the habit of writing simple sentences, using simple words. Lord Denning's short sentence prose in his often mischievous judgements offers students a good example of the effective use of short sentences. Reference all your sources and provide a bibliography at the end. Give accurate citations of cases and statutory provisions. Case law should always be underlined.

Essays

Good essay structure is another key element of competent written work. Each of your answers should contain:

1. an introduction
2. a substantive answer – case law, facts analysis and cogent argument
3. a conclusion – summarising or giving advice, as called for by the question.

This simple but effective structure makes for disciplined arguments, themed issues and logical thought development. Appropriate paragraphing will also help your reader and marker to understand your answers and analysis.

Before handing in your finished piece of work, proofread it meticulously. Consult your College's rules or guidelines on the submission and presentation of written work, to make sure that it adheres to such regulations. Pay particular attention to word limits. Once you feel comfortable and satisfied with your draft, write out a final version of the work and submit it to the appropriate office or person before the deadline.

Above all, never hurry your assignments. Always listen carefully to feedback from your tutors regarding your previous written work, as a further aid to improving performance

Assessment and examinations

All students dread examinations. Though they are often felt to be a terrifying ordeal, you should look upon your assessments as a challenge, and a chance to monitor your progress.

There are various methods of assessment:

1. Unseen open-book examinations. Here you can use your own materials and/or a selected (usually unmarked copy) text, normally a set of statutes.

2. Seen examinations. You prepare your answers in advance, but

scribe down your answers under examination conditions and within set time limits.

3. Multiple choice tests, used to assess memorised knowledge. See Hannibal & Hardy, *MCTs in Constitutional & Administrative Law*, Blackstone Press, for an example. These are very useful to students for revision purposes.

4. Viva voce examinations (oral examinations). These are used more at postgraduate level and for higher degrees.

5. Continuous assessment – phased tests used to assess a student's knowledge of a specific area of law.

All of these seek to probe the depth of your knowledge and your ability to apply the law.

Revision

Revision for examinations should always be well planned and realistic. Cramming is not recommended. Do your revision at times and in places which suit your personal needs.

Of equal importance and idiosyncratic is the method you choose. A contemporary of mine used case names written onto bits of paper which he placed in a tin and drew out at random. He would then recite the facts and the *ratio decidendi* of each case. It sounds a rather tedious method, but for him it was very effective and gave him confidence during his revision.

Many other methods exist. Devise your own and select only the ones you feel really comfortable with. You may, for instance, decide to revise in groups or pairs. Sleep and rest should always complement revision. Choosing what to revise is also a matter of individual preference. Some students choose to revise everything, whilst others cherry pick, or practise using previous examination questions (a very useful pre-examination exercise), or even select areas at random or on the advice of their tutor. At revision time you will be relying heavily upon your notes, so good note-taking is imperative.

In the exam room

When sitting the examination, try to remain calm and relaxed (easier said than done, of course) and keep an eye on the examination clock. Before starting to write an answer, read all of the questions and instructions carefully. Then select the questions which you feel you can tackle best, and draw up short plans of your answers. Then you can start writing your actual answers. Do your best; you can do no more.

Types of question

Law assessment questions

Assessment questions are of two kinds:

1. essay questions
2. problem-based questions

Essay questions

Essay questions seek to test your knowledge base, and your ability to critically evaluate legal concepts, provisions or principles. They require you to define and describe the legal issue, apply it to the question posed, and reach a reasoned conclusion. Take this example:

> 'British subjects are not citizens, because the UK has no written constitution. Discuss.'

This is looking for you to define the terms 'citizen' and 'subject', and then explain the differences between written and unwritten constitutions. You should then discuss the advantages and disadvantages of each type of constitution, and conclude by either agreeing or disagreeing with the statement.

Essay questions typically require you to embark upon an evaluation, appraisal or assessment of a statement, or of some existing legal principle or provision. You will need to demonstrate clear English, good sentence construction, and a structured approach. Back up your answers with well-argued legal discussion, supported by relevant case law and legal provisions.

Whatever the question, essays require you to explore the main issues, using your skills to unravel the complex legal framework containing the question.

Problem questions

In contrast, problem questions aim to test your application and analysis of legal principles. The essential key to answering problem questions is to identify the real legal issues underlying the problem. Next, you must apply the law, accurately and relevantly. As a student I was once told by my tutor that I had adopted a 'scatter-gun' approach to the answering problem questions. For example I had seized on the term 'negligence' in the question and used it as an excuse to write down all I could remember on the law of tort. This was not answering the question.

The primary function of problem-based questions is to set the student a task. This is usually to 'advise X'. When answering problem questions, always tackle the question and complete the task. For instance, 'In conclusion', you should 'advise X' on her/his rights, liabilities, remedies etc... or whatever is called for. All answers to problem-based questions should contain supporting case law and arguments, demonstrating your legal reasoning. Rather as in mathematics, you should aim to write down each stage in your reasoning.

In brief, a satisfactory answer to a problem question will address and answer each part of the question, identify the key legal issues at stake, cite relevant source material in support of the answer, and state and apply the relevant principles of law to the issues discussed.

Students should treat problem questions as a twofold task:

1. Discover the legal issues in dispute.

2. Answer the question, applying only the law which is relevant to the point.

Analysis, accuracy and brevity are the touchstones to success in problem-based questions. To hit the bull's-eye calls for precision. Trying to mow down problem questions with a 'scatter-gun' simply means that you have failed to identify the real target.

Assessment of performance

In law, as in other degree courses, a student's performance is assessed. Generally it is done as follows:

70% + = first class
60% + = second class (upper division)
50% + = second class (lower division)
45% + = third class
40% + = pass

Below 40% is a fail and/or results in the award of an ordinary degree (in other words without Honours). Using this table you can measure your own progress, achievements and success.

A final word

Always remember that legal scholarship has to be earned and learned; it cannot be attained naturally nor without any effort...Good luck in your learning of the law.

Good luck in your studies!

Glossary

Act of parliament A statute, law enacted by the Queen in parliament, or made under delegated powers conferred by statute.

advocate Someone who argues a case, a lawyer, or a legal representative.

adjudication The judicial decision or pronouncement of judgment in a court or tribunal.

Advisory Conciliation and Arbitration Service (ACAS) A government-funded organisation created to offer mediation and conciliation for industrial disputes.

amicus curiae 'Friend of the court'. This is a role which may carried out by the Official Solicitor on behalf of those unable to represent or help themselves (children, wards of court, the mentally ill for example).

Appeal Court The court which hears appeals from the High Court or crown courts.

appellant Person making an appeal from the decision of a lower court.

appellate court judges See Lord Justices of Appeal.

arbitration A procedure in which the parties in a dispute refer the issue to a third party for resolution, rather than take the case to law.

Attorney General The most senior law officer in the UK. A cabinet member, he represents the government or 'the crown', and is responsible for the Director of Public Prosecutions, the Crown Prosecution Service, and the Serious Fraud Office.

Bar, the The collective term for barristers.

barrister A lawyer entitled to appear in any court, including all the higher courts, on behalf of a client.

benchers These were the most senior practising barristers and/or judges. The benchers were responsible for establishing good standards of professional practice at the Bar and within the four

Inns of Court.

Bill Proposed legislation. If a Bill passes through parliament, and receives the royal assent, it becomes an Act of Parliament, and part of the law of the land.

case law The law determined and refined by the courts; the common law.

chambers (or **set of chambers**) A collective of self-employed barristers who share premises, the services of a clerk and other facilities.

Chancery Division of the High Court Division of the High Court which deals with commercial cases.

circuit A group of courts covering a particular region. There are six main circuits in England and Wales: the Midland and Oxford, Northern, North Eastern, Wales and Chester, Western, and South Eastern circuits

circuit judge A judge who sits in a circuit court, travelling from one to the next over a period of weeks.

civil law Civil law regulates the legal relationships between individuals. This area of law, for examples, covers contracts, property and land, commercial activities, employment and probate (involving wills and property).

common law The term that came to be used for the laws and customs applied by the royal courts which emerged after the Norman Conquest (1066), and which progressively replaced local laws and customs applied in sundry local courts.

constitutional and administrative law This category of law concerns the regulation of government activities and governs the law relating to abuse of power by the holders of state control.

county court A district court which determines civil disputes between parties.

court The place in which a judge dispenses justice.

criminal law This law relates to the conduct between the state and individuals. Criminal law is therefore about the enforcement of particular patterns of behaviour. In sociological terms, the criminal law is the mechanism by which the state can impose control upon its citizens.

crown, the The monarch, symbolic head of the legal authority of the state.

crown court A judge and jury determine the guilt or innocence of defendants charged with serious criminal offences.

custody Detention in prison or some other secure institution.

defendant Person required to attend court to answer a case brought by a plaintiff (civil case) or the crown (criminal prosecution).

delegated powers See **statutory instrument**.

Director of Public Prosecutions Answerable to the Attorney-General, this law officer is responsible for the day-to-day conduct of the Crown Prosecution Service and the Serious Fraud Office.

directions hearing At this hearing the district judge ascertains the facts from each party and enquires as to whether the matter can be settled. If not, a date for trial is set.

district judges Part-time judges sitting in the county courts.

enact To make law, to pass an Act of parliament.

European Commission The permanent body of officials of the European Union. It is not unlike the UK civil service. It consists of twenty commissioners, each a representative of a member state. Their role is to initiate and draft legislation and to enforce it where they have power to do so

European Council The forum in which the heads of government, namely prime ministers or presidents of the member states, meet to discuss policy matters.

European Court of Justice The legal institution of the European Union. It consists of the Court of First Instance (for competition cases and internal staff matters) and the Court of Justice itself. Its chief role is to interpret and uphold the Treaty.

European Parliament The democratically elected organ of the European Union. This institution is composed of 624 directly elected members (MEPs) from fifteen member states.

European Union Consists of 15 member states administering common social, economic and national policies.

ex officio By virtue of holding office.

Family Division of the High Court A civil appeal court which considers matrimonial and domestic cases.

Gray's Inn One of the four Inns of Court to which barristers belong.

habeas corpus A writ ordering a person to be brought before a court or judge, especially so that the court may ascertain whether the detention is lawful.

High Court Is an appeal court with both civil and criminal jurisdiction, divided into three divisions: Queen's Bench, Chancery and Family.

Home Secretary Member of the cabinet responsible for law and order, the police, prisons, immigration and other matters of social order.

Incorporated Council of Law Reporting The body responsible since 1865 for cataloguing law reports in the UK.

Inner Temple One of the four Inns of Court to which barristers belong.

Inns of Court

judge The public adjudicator in a court of law.

judicial review A High Court action seeking to challenge the decision of a public authority.

Judicial Studies Board An organisation which trains judges.

judiciary The collective term for the persons appointed to adjudicate in courts or tribunals upon disputes.

junior Term for a barrister who assists a Queen's Counsel in a court case.

jurisprudence The so-called philosophy of law. It presents many theories on the nature of law.

justice of the peace Magistrate.

justices' clerks These are legally trained or qualified magistrates' courtroom advisers and administrators. They are responsible for the administration of court business, in other words its procedures, and act as legal advisers to the bench of lay magistrates (the justices of the peace).

juvenile court A section of the magistrates court, which deals with criminal prosecutions of young persons under the age of 18.

law Long-established system of enforceable principles and rules which govern the dealings and behaviour of people in relation to the state and to each other.

Law Commission A permanent, independent advisory body whose function is to review the current law and make recommendations.

law lords The most senior judges in the UK. They are members of the House of Lords and comprise the highest court within the

UK jurisdiction.

legal aid Government/tax payer funding of legal services for those litigants who cannot afford their own means.

Lincoln's Inn One of the four Inns of Court to which barristers belong.

litigation Proceedings in a civil court. The litigants are the plaintiff and the defendant.

Lord Chancellor The highest judicial office holder in the UK, responsible for the administration of the courts, supervision of legal aid and judicial appointments.

Lord Chief Justice A senior judge who is head/presides over the criminal courts in the UK.

Lord Justices of Appeal More widely known as appellate court judges, there are thirty-five of these. Normally the Appeal Court judges are practitioners of over ten years' standing, and already sitting as High Court judges.

magistrate Justice of the peace, adjudicator in the lowest level of court. Most magistrates are lay volunteers, though stipendiary (paid) magistrates serve in the major urban areas.

maladministration A situation in which the performance of a government department, local authority, European institution, or other public service has fallen below an acceptable standard. The failure may be characterised by 'neglect, bias, delay, incompetence, arbitrariness, perversity and turpitude'.

mandatory Compulsory, required by law.

Master of the Rolls

'McKenzie's friend' In British courts the term refers to any unqualified person who may speak for a defendant or plaintiff lacking legal representation.

mediation The process in which a third party acts as the conduit through which two parties in dispute communicate in an attempt to resolve a problem.

MEP Members of the European Parliament.

metropolitan stipendiary magistrate A stipendiary magistrate whose court is in London or one of the major provincial cities.

Middle Temple One of the four Inns of Court to which barristers belong.

moot A mock trial. Used as a model of legal teaching/training.

natural justice Collective term used to describe the central requirements of impartiality and a right to a fair hearing.

obiter dictum 'Spoken aside', words spoken by a judge as an aside, and not forming part of his main judgment.

Official Solicitor A senior law officer and lawyer of 10 years' standing. He is responsible for bail matters, representing wards of court, conducting litigation for children and mental patients, administering the intestate estates of deceased persons, and acting as *amicus curiae* ('friend of the court').

ombudsperson An official to whom complaints or grievances can be addressed. The word is Swedish in origin and means 'representative of the people'.

parliamentary counsel Civil servants who translate political objectives into draft legal form.

parole A prisoner's right to early release for 'good behaviour'.

plaintiff Someone who brings an action against a defendant in a civil court.

primary legislation Legislation that is enacted by Parliament.

Private Bill A proposed piece of legislation dealing with something which may not be a matter of huge public concern, but which still requires enactment by parliament. For example, it may be required for a major public planning project, or the granting of a licence.

private law The legal relationships between individual citizens is categorised as private law. Civil law is a category of private law.

Private Member's Bill A proposed piece of legislation presented by an individual MP on issue where he or she wishes to amend the law. These Bills are often derived from the work of pressure groups.

Public Bill A proposed piece of legislation normally presented, if not supported, by the government.

Privy Council Represents a body of appointees who consider matters in relation to the former British colonies. Its judicial committee hears appeals from former British colonies' courts.

procurators The term for a prosecutor in the Scottish courts.

public law Public law concerns the relationship between the citizen and the state. This law involves the regulation of state power. Criminal law is an example of public law. Since the 1980s, however, public law largely describes the area of law called constitutional and administrative law, which concerns the regulation of government activities and governs the law relating to abuse of power by the holders of state control.

puisne judges The historical Latin name for High Court judges, derived from the fact that they travelled from place to place to administer justice.

Queen's Bench Division A division of the High Court dealing with contractual and taxation claims, and criminal appeals.

Queen's Counsel Are letters patent given to identify the most senior practitioners of the Bar.

ratio decidendi 'The reason for deciding'. This reason can be any rule of law which may guide a judge and jury in reaching a decision.

recorders Part-time crown court judges. They are appointed to sit in a specific court for a fixed duration and number of days. Recorders usually have ten or more years' practice, and serve as recorders for three years at a time.

Royal Commissions These are an *ad hoc* mechanism constituted by government to investigate the need for reform, and to make appropriate recommendations.

secondary (delegated) legislation See **statutory instrument.**

sentence Punishment meted out by a judge or magistrate to a person convicted in criminal proceedings, usually in the form of a fine, probation, term of imprisonment or community service.

silk Colloquial term for a barrister who is a Queen's Counsel.

solicitor A qualified lawyer who is a member of the Law Society.

Solicitor General A law officer and member of the government of the day.

sovereignty Loosely means the authority to make and unmake laws.

Speaker The Queen's official representative in the House of Commons. The Speaker acts as a kind of chair of the proceedings.

stare decisis – 'Keep to what has been decided previously'. The principle of binding precedent in which the lower courts are bound by the decisions of the higher courts.

statute An Act of Parliament.

statute book The general term referring to all legislation currently in force and enacted by parliament.

statutory instrument Secondary or delegated legislation. This refers to the powers under which a Minister, the Secretary of State responsible, or their civil servants (acting in *alter ego*) can draft and enact, under the powers given to the relevant Minister under a particular Act of Parliament.

stipendiary magistrate A professional paid magistrate, as distinct from a lay magistrate.

tagging A telephonic monitoring system which relays information about an offender's location and conduct

tortious Relating to tort, a civil wrong.

white paper A public discussion document produced by government for testing the opinions of those affected, or likely to be affected, by a proposed reform.

Index